Praise

Gifford Pinchot and the Old Timers

American history was changed forever—and for better—by the generations who took the reins in the early twentieth century. Amid the turbulence of our new century, we can draw actionable inspiration from Gifford Pinchot and the Old Timers who created the U.S. Forest Service. Bibi Gaston has compiled their words into timeless traits of character. She makes clear that we are all descendants and beneficiaries of these courageous, intrepid individuals. Gaston challenges us to reach for a comparable legacy. With this field guide, we're equipped for the journey.

—James Strock, founding Secretary,
California Environmental Protection Agency,
author, Theodore Roosevelt on Leadership

Conservationists and lovers of our national forests will find this fascinating reading. Gifford Pinchot left many gifts for future generations. Among those gifts were his philosophy of conservation, our country's national forests and the forestry profession itself. these letters from the Old Timers are also a remarkable gift. they are a window to the past that help us appreciate where we are today. Hopefully, they will give us courage to do what's right for future generations.

—Dale Bosworth, Former Chief, U.S. Forest Service

What a marvelous book Bibi Gaston has created about her great-grand-uncle Gifford Pinchot, Chief Forester of the U.S. Forest Service from 1905–1909, and all his fellow forestry pioneers. Not only is it fascinating history but also inspiration for our current desperate efforts to save the planet's remaining precious, carbon-absorbing trees and the rest of beleaguered nature—without which we and countless other species cannot survive for much longer. Pinchot's idea says it all: Conservation is the basis of permanent peace. As we honor our environmental ancestors, they provide us with the courage and inspiration to do what must be done.

—Linda Buzzell, co-editor, Ecotherapy: Healing with Nature in Mind
(Sierra Club Books, 2009)

With Gifford Pinchot and the First Foresters, Bibi Gaston has given us a special gift. Historians were aware of a collection of letters that passed between Gifford Pinchot, Teddy Roosevelt's chief forester, and the Old Timers, the hard-working rangers of the early days of the U.S. Forest Service. Those letters, however, remained inaccessible, buried deep in archival collections. Until now. In this volume Gaston brings forward these vivid voices of American conservation history—as reminders of their commitment to public service in their own time, and as welcome calls to democratic reengagement in ours.

—Curt Meine, Senior Fellow,
Aldo Leopold Foundation/Center for Humans and Nature
Author, Aldo Leopold: His Life and Work

Bibi Gaston has unearthed a treasure of short memories by many, here-to-fore little known men and women whose collective efforts began the great conservation model—the United States Forest Service. She may also have provided the spark for a renewed conservation program that provides employment, restoration to forests, and the early "can-do" spirit.

—Chad Oliver, Pinchot Professor of Forestry and Environmental Studies,
and Director, Global Institute of Sustainable Forestry School of Forestry
and Environmental Studies, Yale University

Bibi Gaston's treasure-trove of reflections from the early years of the US Forest Service brings to life how Gifford Pinchot's vision of "the greatest good for the greatest number in the long run" was made real through the hard work, integrity, and sacrifice of a small but dedicated group of "Old Timers." is book shows us that their values helped shape America in the early years of last century, and it reminds us of the importance of those same values for helping us find our way in the next.

—Sir Peter Crane FRS Dean,
Yale School of Forestry & Environmental Studies

Gifford Pinchot
and the
Old Timers

VOLUME 1

BIBI GASTON

Gifford Pinchot
and the
Old Timers

VOLUME 1

BIBI GASTON

Baked Apple Club Productions
New Milford, Connecticut

Copyright ©2018 Patricia Gaston
All rights reserved.

Printed in the United States of America.
Baked Apple Club Productions, LLC
New Milford, Connecticut

First Printing

Names: Gaston, Patricia, 1959-author.
Title: Gifford Pinchot and The Old Timers
ISBN 978-0-9972162-1-9

Material in this book includes excerpted correspondence between Gifford Pinchot and a select group of former U.S. Forest Service employees he called the Old Timers. These men and women responded to his request for personal narratives to be preserved at the Library of Congress with the understanding that their stories would be included in a book about the history of the Forest Service. To the best of our knowledge the material included in this collection is available for publication in the manner that Gifford Pinchot intended.

Additional copies can be purchased through our website at bibigaston.com

Photo Credits: Cover: Gifford Pinchot portrait: the Gerald Williams Collection at Oregon State University. Page 15: Annual meeting of the Society of American Foresters, Oct 18, 1915. Panama Pacific International Exposition, San Francisco. By P. Cardinell-Vincent Co. Offcial Photographers. Courtesy of Library of Congress Manuscript Division, Gifford Pinchot Collection. Photo page 10 from the Gerald Williams Collection at Oregon State University. Author photo: Rebecca Hammel. Photographs in this book courtesy of the Library of Congress Manuscript Division, Gifford Pinchot Collection.

Book design by Colleen Sheehan
Book layout by David Provolo

Publisher's Cataloging-In-Publication Data (Prepared by The Donohue Group, Inc.)
Names: Gaston, Bibi
Title: Gifford Pinchot and the Old Timers.
Description: New Milford, Connecticut : Baked Apple Club Productions, LLC,
    [2018] | Includes bibliographical references.
Identifiers: ISBN 978-0-9972162-1-9
Subjects: LCSH: Pinchot, Gifford B.--Correspondence. | Foresters--United
    States--Correspondence. | Communication in forestry--United
States-- History--
    20th century. | Forests and forestry--United States--History--20th century. |
    Conservation of natural resources--United States--History--20th century. |
    Correspondence.
Classification: LCC SD127 .G54 2016 | DDC 634.90922--dc23

For The Old Timers of the U.S. Forest Service

Contents

Preface

DISCOVERING THE OLD TIMERS

"Of the greatest consequence was this—every member of the Service realized that it was engaged in a great and necessary undertaking in which the whole future of their country was at stake. The Service had a clear understanding of where it was going, it was determined to get there, and it was never afraid to fight for what was right." [1]

They hailed from the Sandhills of Nebraska, the small farms of Iowa, and one-stop towns from Maine to Tennessee. They were called "Old Timers" not because they were old but because they'd seen and done and endured things the rest of us can hardly imagine. The term "Old Timers" was one of respect. They were to be revered.

Between the years 1905 and 1910, before the advent of GPS, tracking devices, or accurate maps, 226 men and several women made their way to their posts in the Western United States. Most were in their twenties and thirties but some were still in their teens. Some walked, others boarded the train, and many rode on a saddlehorse while porting their gear on a packhorse they bought themselves. They were paid $60 a month to "grow up with the country," bring order to chaos, string telephone lines, tame the range wars, keep records and notes about trees, plants,

---

[1] Pinchot, Gifford. Breaking New Ground. (Washington, D.C: Island Press, 2009). 285.

people they met, and places they went. They cruised vast stands of timber and tamped down the embers of fast-moving wildfires. The men who hired them, Gifford Pinchot, first Chief of the U.S. Forest Service and Theodore Roosevelt, 26th President of the United States, insisted that they were working for the benefit of America, not for them. Roosevelt, the "Conservation President" and Pinchot, "Chief Forester," placed some 230 million acres of land under federal protection on behalf of the American people. They placed their trust, and no small trust it was, in the men and women in the field, the Old Timers, to protect it.

In 1937, some thirty years after the Old Timers had left their posts, and twenty years after Roosevelt's death, Gifford Pinchot sat down at an old wooden desk at 1615 Rhode Island Avenue in Washington, D.C. to write a letter to each of them. Most of them he knew personally. He addressed some by their last name. Each showed a dedication and fortitude he would never forget. To many his letter came as a surprise because they thought their job was over and done, but he had one more favor to ask: he wanted their stories. He wanted to know what they remembered of their time in the Forest Service, what obstacles they had encountered, what battles lost and won, and why they had chosen forestry as a profession. Each was humble and could hardly imagine that their testimonials would amount to anything. But Pinchot wouldn't take no for an answer. There was integrity in the simplest job well done.

So they took pen in hand and wrote for the sake of the good old days and their "Old Chief." Love letters of a sort, letters

President Theodore Roosevelt and Chief Forester Gifford Pinchot on the river steamer Mississippi during a meeting of the Inland Waterways Commission in October 1907. — Library of Congress (1907-01-01)

of respect and gratitude. What Gifford Pinchot and Theodore Roosevelt had given them were the greatest gifts one could give: meaningful work, a sense of purpose, companionship, and the greatest adventure of their lives.

By the time Pinchot wrote his letter in the summer of 1937, some of the Old Timers had died. Some were still working, but most had retired and had time on their hands. They wrote 5, 25, sometimes 150 pages, and they wrote as if it was yesterday. They sent diaries, scrapbooks, poetry, photographs, dramatic scripts, and ballads. They sent images of the first fire lookout stations, a final encounter with Buffalo Bill Cody, and sowing Doug fir seeds on the snow-covered slopes of Mt. Hood. They sent photos of themselves and of their families who had struggled and sacrificed alongside them. They responded with accounts of chasing and being chased by bears and mountain lions and clinging to the sides of cliffs with a bedroll and a handkerchief. They sent accounts of losing a horse and walking for three days. One forester's wife sent an account of losing two children and then her husband. The foresters sent all of it. And for their old Chief, none of it was too much.

Pinchot's admiration for them was boundless and for each he had words of encouragement and gratitude for what they had done, not for him, but for the American people. But it was Frothingham whose words called out to me like music in the forest. His was the voice of Whitman, Roosevelt, Leopold, and Muir, embodied in a simple sentence. His words were innocence in amber. "I owe my first inclination towards forestry," wrote Ranger

Annual meeting of The Society of American Foresters, Oct 18, 1915.
Panama Pacific International Exposition, San Francisco.
By P. Cardinell-Vincent Co. Official Photographers. Courtesy of Library of Congress.
Manuscript Division. Gifford Pinchot Collection.

Earl H. Frothingham from Biltmore Forest, North Carolina in the summer of 1940, "to an early passion for the study of birds."

One of the Old Timers that Pinchot trained was Aldo Leopold whom the author Wallace Stegner called a prophet. Leopold responded to the old Chief's call with a brief letter. It is unknown if he sent a narrative. He did, however, make a prediction regarding Pinchot's collection of stories: "Perhaps a generation or two must elapse," he wrote, "before its values can be truly weighed by anyone."

Leopold's timing was just about right. Two generations had elapsed and America was ready for stories that might rekindle the spirit and put a fire under us to act, not separately but together. Here was a different kind of story, not a story of the great man or the great event, but a narrative of, by, and for the people. Here were 226 unknown men and women whose work in the woods, on the planes, and in the desert made it possible to live the lives we do and who held a mirror to our deepest selves. Here were men and women we could be proud of, whose words matched their deeds, and who were humble, grateful, and full of anticipation for the America that was yet to be. Here was a reason to fall in love all over again with the dream of America.

For nearly 80 years, it seemed, the Old Timers' stories had disappeared. Perhaps they hadn't disappeared so much as been buried in the two million-document Pinchot Collection at the Manuscript Division in the Library of Congress. That is where I found them. For years I visited the Old Timers as if I was returning home. Their stories and photographs brought me back to a self who, at 29, traveled West to restore derelict places, reclaim quarry sites, and rebuild part of America's historic highway system, parks, forests, overlooks, trails, and shelters. I'd dug up the past and with it a sense of purpose.

The Old Timers took the difficult road. In 1905, practically no one knew what a professional forester was or why a trained and tested cadre of men wearing military uniforms and badges should be sent out like satellites into the remote reaches of America. But Pinchot knew: conserving America's resources meant not just conserving her water, trees, and land, but finding the individuals who were committed to conservation and putting them to work.

The Old Timers weren't Republicans, Democrats, or Independents. Their old Chief was a conservative, committed to the true meaning of conservative which meant to conserve resources for the future, not to waste, plunder, or overspend. He was indifferent to party. It was people that mattered and the American people needed to put an end to the range wars, save the land from marauders, protect wildlife and water, replant the forests, halt erosion, and bring order to the West.

Pinchot knew that the future would contain shards of the past, so he engaged the best of the past in order to move forward. In 1905 America needed to re-invent itself. We'd forgotten who we were. We needed a new narrative.

One hundred years after a band of 226 of America's first foresters set out for their posts and offices, I started photographing five thousand pages of correspondence at the Library of Congress. For weeks on end I sat gripping a camera, turning pages, and thinking I had discovered the Holy Grail. Several years later, I sat down to read the Old Timers letters at a drafting board in France. My mother read to me as a child, so I took a summer to read to myself. I'd found Abbey from California and Abbot from Montana and Blake from Oregon, but it was Frothingham from, well, it was hard to say where he was from exactly, who reassured me that the America of the Old Timers wasn't gone, it was just forgotten. Discovering the Old Timer narratives changed the course of my life. I believed they would change the course of my country's future forever.

Grey Towers designed by architect Richard Morris Hunt showing deforested landscape. Circa 1886.

Dear Old-Timer:

The record of how the Forest Service was born, fought, con-
quered, and grew up is of national importance and surely ought
to be preserved in full. I want to do what I can toward assuring
that the story of what we did, what we faced, and why, gets told
straight; and I am trying to put down what I know about it and
what I had to do with it, with the idea of printing it in a book.
In this undertaking I need and very much want the help of all
old-timers.

Many of those who were in the Service during my time have
already been of immense assistance. They have sent me personal
narratives telling what each one did and saw, what they and the
Service were up against, and what they thought about it. The
result is a composite account of the Service that I am finding
invaluable.

But that is not all. Taken together, the narratives are of
almost unbelievable historical value. I want to make the collection as complete as possible, so that the story of the Service
may never be lost. What they send in not only will help me with
my book, but also will be permanently preserved, with other
similar historical material in my possession, in the Library
of Congress. Your personal experience should be made a part of
this record.

In your story I hope you will describe the positions you
have filled, your duties in each, the names of the persons and
places, descriptions of early conditions, and anecdotes -- all
that you possibly can. And especially dates, so that what you
send can be combined with the accounts of others.

Above all, I want a picture of your work year by year, told in
your own way, and of the conditions under which it was done,
the difficulties you had to face, the opposition or cooperation
you met, and from whom, the friendly or hostile public sentiment at the time, and if it changed, what made it change. In fact
you cannot give me anything I will not be glad to have. I hope

that you will give me the reason or influence that made you go into forestry.

Furthermore, I shall be immensely grateful for any information you can give me concerning collections of personal papers of your own or present or former members of the Forest service--letters, diaries or whatever else--that would properly form part of the historical material that will go to the Library of Congress for permanent preservation.

I thank you most heartily in advance for your help to your old Chief, who sends you his best appreciation and regards.

Gifford Pinchot,
Milford, Pennsylvania.[2]

---

2 Gifford Pinchot produced numerous drafts of his letter to the Old Timers. The first extant is to be found in 1937 and was placed as an advertisement in the Journal of Forestry.

Gifford Pinchot was born in Simsbury, Connecticut on August 11, 1865, the son of James Pinchot and Mary Jane Eno. Both the Pinchots and the Enos were noted for their public-mindedness, active engagement, and civic contributions. In 1886, when Gifford was 21 years old, his parents embarked on an ambitious construction project, a new summer "cottage," Grey Towers, in Milford, Pennsylvania, designed by Gilded Age architect Richard Morris Hunt. Built from local materials and clad in Pennsylvania schist, Grey Towers was paid for by the family's success in their New York City wallpaper business, Pinchot and Warren. Earlier generations of the Pinchot family had logged portions of the property and floated the cut down the Delaware River to ports in New Jersey and Pennsylvania. At the time Grey Towers was constructed, much of the surrounding forest had been cut down and the land resembled a moonscape.

James and Mary Pinchot had sizeable ambitions for their eldest son. With a fascination for trees, gardens, and civic improvement, and connections in New York social and political circles, James Pinchot was determined that Gifford should become a leader in the profession of forestry. By the time the Pinchots endowed the Yale School of Forestry in 1900, restoring the nation's depleted woodlands had become a national imperative for Theodore Roosevelt and others who saw the connection between forests and rivers, between forests and industry, between forests and an individual's relationship to nature and community. Fortunately, the Pinchots knew the Roosevelts. Through their timely connection, a new era of conservation was born.

Today, as we contemplate the loss of forests and species, the Old Timer narratives might lead us to despair. After all, we were warned. Pinchot and Roosevelt weren't afraid to point a finger at the culprits: human greed and destructiveness. Nor did they hesitate to charge into action. After decades of denial, it is instructive to recall an era of innovation and cooperation in which young citizen-conservationists worked in dedicated and joyful service to the environment.

The Atlantic Building C. 1933.
Credit: Library of Congress, Prints & Photographs Division, HABS,
Reproduction number HABS DC, WASH, 655A—1

chapter 1

Bertha E. Adams
WASHINGTON, D.C.
1891-1912

"I could not then realize that destiny had placed me in a position where my early environment would help me to visualize much that was connected with the work I was called upon to do."

—Bertha E. Adams

When I imagine Bertha E. Adams, I see her sitting at her desk wondering how she might best serve her family, her workplace, and her country. She was one of a small number of women who responded to the Old Chief's call for letters. Her position was classified as "stenographer-typist." She was responsible for keeping detailed records of who, what, where, when, and how the Agency did what it did with the meager resources appropriated by Congress.

Bertha Adams reported to work each day in a room known as "The Rose Garden" on the sixth floor of the eight-story Atlantic Building at 930 F Street in Washington, D.C. where the Forest Service established its headquarters in 1906. When it was completed in 1888, the Atlantic Building was the largest commercial structure in the city and came equipped with its own passenger elevator, one of Washington's first. The Atlantic had two large assembly rooms where public meetings were held, including one at which the National Zoo was founded. In 1890, the eighth floor served as headquarters for President Benjamin Harrison's inaugural committee.[1]

Bertha Adams provides us with a short but detailed account of her day-to-day work in the fight for conservation. She made the best of every day, serving the American people in a field of work that was barely known in 1905: forestry. Thirty years after her service, we learn how she saw the world and her role in it.

With the 1906 transfer of duties from the corrupt General Land Office, part of the Department of the Interior, to the newly-minted U.S. Forest Service, part of the Department of Agriculture, Pinchot penned a new chapter in land management and government organization. To separate itself from the past, he and his leadership team created a system of record-keeping that kept government accountable. Keeping records had another purpose: training a generation of young people in accounting and bookkeeping. Bertha Adams did not go West to "grow up with the country" like most of her male counterparts. She was assigned to record-keeping, a part of the mission Pinchot knew to be critical to the Agency's success.

My mother, would-be attorney Frances Clothilde Loud Gaston, spent most of her life as a paralegal and a typist. She started out as one of the first women at Harvard Law School. Some said she was destined for the Supreme Court, but by a series of conscious and unconscious decisions and a lack of support, her extraordinary gifts and destiny failed to materialize. Judging by

1 http://wikimapia.org/978517/The-Atlantic-Building

what I'd seen of my mother's typing prowess, I imagine she and Bertha Adams would have become fast friends, swapping tips and taking their brown bag lunches to sit on a bench in the sun. In their world, spelling and punctuation were important, but it was friendship, curiosity, kindness, and duty that mattered most.

Great men built this nation. Gifford Pinchot also knew that great women had staffed and supported the agencies that made the mens' work possible. After he crafted his request for Old Timer narratives, Pinchot often followed up imploring the foresters to send the stories of their wives. He received numerous responses that pointed to the central role of women in accomplishing field and office work. Whether man or woman, whether tasked with accounting, surveying, or patrolling 500,000 acres, work in the Forest Service required accuracy and reliability.

Bertha Adams sent her narrative from her home in Rockville, Maryland. On April 16, 1940 she wrote: "I have no typewriter, therefore this story is submitted in handwriting, purposely on ruled paper to facilitate copying by your secretary, if perchance it has any value for your purpose. If so, may I ask that you send me a carbon copy of the part you use? I shall consider it an honor to have any testimony of mine filed with your memoirs in the Congressional Library."

Thirty years after Bertha Adams served as a stenographer-typist, her skills were still intact. We might ask: what was the secret to her success? The answer: accuracy, reliability, kindness, courtesy, and respect.

Bertha Adams had typed every Presidential land proclamation between 1891 and 1900. Did she know that she was essential to the mission? Today we might think she should have aspired to a more competitive position. While Gifford admonished his rangers: "a forester is not a politician," a public servant is a goodwill ambassador, accountable to his or her nation. Bertha Adams did her job because of us, on behalf of us. She relied on her Oliver typewriter. She also relied on her mind. For her we have ample reason to be proud.

Edson Lane
Rockville, Md.
January 30, 1940.

Dear Mr. Pinchot:

Your letter of January 9 was received on the 27th, and since then I have been thinking whether I can write any thing of much value for the matter you intend to place in the Congressional Library pertaining to your part in the Forest Service. I was only a "cog in the wheel," but it was my good fortune to be placed in that position almost immediately after my appointment as a stenographer and typist on November 18, 1890, and then, three months later, the Act of March 3, 1891, authorizing the creation of Forest Reserves, was passed. I was so inexperienced in the facts that led up to this that I did not realize its great potential importance for some time. However, the story unfolded and eventuated in my transfer to the Forest Service on February 1, 1905—an eventful day for me, and I hope that I may be able to record my part in this history of the movement in a way that may be of some worth. I shall try to do this as soon as I can and forward it to you.

I thank you heartily for your invitation to have a part in this important matter.

Sincerely yours
Bertha E. Adams

Hon. Gifford Pinchot
1615 Rhode Island Ave. N.W.
Washington, D.C.

1615 Rhode Island Ave. N. W.
Washington, D. C.

February 6, 1940

Miss Bertha E. Adams,
Edson Lane,
Rockville, Maryland.

Dear Miss Adams:

I am delighted to know that you
are going to write your story, and I shall
look forward to it with the greatest
interest. Take your time about it. If I
can have it by the first of April or May,
that will be fine.

With every good wish and high
appreciation,

Faithfully yours,

GP

GP: AMB

Edson Lane,
Rockville, Md.

April 16, 1940.

Hon. Gifford Pinchot,
1615 Rhode Island Ave., N.W.,
Washington D.C.

Dear Mr. Pinchot:

Referring to your letters of January 9 and
February 6, 1940, I am enclosing herewith the "story" of
my connection with the forestry movement in the United
States.

I might have included more of the details of my
service, but feel that the conditions so clearly described
by Mr. Smith-Riley in his narrative dated March 12,
1912- with which I was familiar- require no more than my
confirmation.

I have no typewriter, therefore the story is
submitted in handwriting, purposely, on ruled paper to
facilitate copying by your secretary, if, perchance, it has
any value for your purpose. If so, may I ask that you send
me a carbon copy of the part you may use?

I shall consider it an honor to have any
testimony of mine filed with your memoirs in the
Congressional Library.

Thanking you and with all best wishes,

Sincerely yours,
Bertha E. Adams

p 4 7 9 13

The Personal Narrative of
Miss Bertha E. Adams
April 16. 1940.

November 18, 1890, as the result
of a Civil Service examination, I was
appointed a Stenographer and Typist—
in the General Land Office, a Bureau
of the Interior Department, Washington,
D.C. I could not then realize
that destiny had placed me
in a position where my early
environment would help me
to visualize much that was
connected with the work I was
called upon to do. My forebears
came from New England as pioneers
to western New York when it was

From the handwritten narrative of Bertha E. Adams.
Library of Congress. Manuscript Division.
Gifford Pinchot Collection. Old Timers Collection.

a wilderness inhabited by Indians and wild animals. Pioneering was in their blood, and ere long, some of them pushed farther west into the wilderness of Ohio, Michigan, and Wisconsin. Then, later, cousins slightly older than myself went to Iowa and Nebraska to do their parts in the settlement of those regions. In time one, an aunt, returned to New York State and very vivid is my memory of her accounts of their struggles in trying to make homes in those then far-away places. The story thrilled me. Those early settlers were tillable-land-hungry. Therefore, they considered the forests as liabilities rather than assets, since they possessed nothing but their brawn and muscle to clear the land. On the other hand those who went to the plains region wished there were trees there with which to build log houses instead of making them with sod, but they had scant or no means of communicating with their people back East and telling them that they had come to know the values of forests. So time went on until it was discovered that our priceless inheritance was being destroyed to such an extent as to alarm certain public-spirited people, and a movement began which resulted in the passage by Congress of the Act of March 3, 1891 authorizing the creation of the "Forest Reserves." Previously, however, under an act dated September 1, 1890, the first reserve was created in California, which covered some of the area now within the Sierra National Forest.

Promptly after March 3, 1891 President Harrison established a forest reserve covering lands lying to the east of the Yellowstone National Park. An addition to that reserve was made on September 10, 1891. Thereafter, President Harrison proclaimed several reserves as follows:

The White River in Colorado, on October 16, 1891;
The Pecos River in New Mexico, on January 11, 1892;

The Pike's Peak in Colorado, on February 11, 1892;
The Bull Run in Oregon, on June 17, 1892;
The Plum Creek in Colorado, on June 23, 1892;
The South Platte in Colorado, on December 9, 1892;
The San Gabriel in California, on December 20, 1892;
The Sierra in California, on February 14, 1893;
The Pacific, in Washington, on February 20, 1893;
The Grand Canyon in Arizona, on February 20, 1893;
The San Bernardino, in California, on February 25, 1893;
The Trabuco Canyon, in California, on February 25, 1893.

President Cleveland proclaimed the Cascade Reserve in Oregon on September 28, 1894 and the Ashland Reserve in southern Oregon on September 28, 1894. Thereafter, no new reserves were proclaimed until near the close of Mr. Cleveland's administration, when there were quite a number proclaimed on February 22, 1897. (I regret that I have not at hand the record of the names of these reserves.) Subsequently, Congress ordered that these proclamations should not take effect until February 22, 1898.

Since from the first, I was one of those designated to assist in this forest reserve work, it fell to my lot to type the final drafts of practically all the proclamations from 1891 to 1900. All told, those proclamations covered reserves in Arizona, California, Colorado, Idaho, Montana, New Mexico, Nevada, North Dakota, Oregon, Utah, and Washington.

The story of the attempted administration of these reserves, and the difficulties encountered is correctly described by Mr. Smith-Riley in his narrative dated March 12, 1912.[2]

2   Smith Riley, referred to by Bertha Adams as Smith-Riley, was one of the first U.S. Forest Service historians. He was assigned to head the Forest Service regional office in Denver, Colorado. See Pinkett, Harold T. "The First Federal Expert in Forest History." Forest and Conservation History, Volume 6, Issue 3, 1 January 1962. Pages 8-10. https://doi.org/10.2307/forhis/6.3.10

Under the Act of Congress of February 1, 1905, the jurisdiction of the Forest Reserves was transferred from the General Land Office to the Forest Service, Department of Agriculture in charge of Mr. Gifford Pinchot. Several of the Land Office clerks, including myself, were transferred at the same time. A different atmosphere was immediately sensed namely that of public service as that referred to in Mr. Smith-Riley's narrative. Under the new regime the name of the Reserves were changed to the National Forests and some considerations, eliminations, and additions were made in the light of further knowledge of the character of the lands and the public interests involved.

At first, appropriations were small for the task that Mr. Pinchot and his co-planners envisioned. Nevertheless, valiant work was done until the great day came, December 1, 1908 when a large part of the records were transferred to the six District headquarters that had been designated in the West, namely:

District One, Missoula, Montana;
District Two, Denver, Colorado;
District Three, Albuquerque, N. Mx;
District Four, Ogden, Utah;
District Five, San Francisco, Calif, and
District Six, Portland, Oregon

The head officer in each District was designated "District Forester" and his organization was practically a duplicate of that of the Washington Office.

This step was the beginning of the dream of the Forest Service to take the work home to the people interested. Naturally, there were local misunderstandings; the private political ideas had to be overcome. However, wise and patient counsel changed prejudice to favor.

I was greatly interested in one experiment by the
Forest Service, a <u>planted</u> forest in the Sandhills of
Nebraska, first named the "Niobrara," but later changed
to the Nebraska National Forest. As I remember, there
were doubts on the part of some as to the possibility of
the success of the undertaking in that treeless region.
Imagine with what interest I read an article in the
Evening Star of Washington, D.C. sometime in October <u>1939</u>
stating that this <u>planted</u> forest had just celebrated its
thirtieth anniversary when people from several states had
journeyed to see the beautiful forest which God and the
intelligence of man had produced.

Necessarily, much of the policy-forming force
remained in the Washington Office after the formation
of the District offices, but a large part of the clerical
force was transferred to the West, but I was one of those
who remained in Washington. The exodus of so many of
the workers to the field necessitated considerable
reorganization, and I was "fitted in" until the early
summer of 1912, when I was placed in charge of the Section
of Stenography and Typewriting, where new appointees
were trained by doing the miscellaneous overflow work
from all of the Branches and Offices, in addition to the
mimeograph work for the whole office. Having charge of
this part of the work afforded me more than the usual
clerical opportunity to become acquainted not only with
the policy-making personnel of the Washington office but
with the field officers who came in on detail from time
to time. Thus, I came to know how the National forestry
movement was constantly growing onward and upward in
the public mind until my retirement in 1929. There is
much more that I could relate which I am sure will be done

by others more competent than myself. I have never lost my keen interest in the work, and the memory of my connection with it and such a public-spirited company of people has greatly enriched my years of separation from it and them.

1615 Rhode Island Ave., N.W.,
Washington, D.C.,
April 18, 1940.

Mrs. Bertha E. Adams,
Edson Lane,
Rockville, Maryland.

Dear Miss Adams:

My very best thanks for your letter
of April 16 and for the very interesting
account of your work in the Forest Service
which accompanied it. I was particularly
interested, for example, to know that under
an act dated September 1, 1890 the first
Forest Reserve was created in California.
That was entirely new to me, and I am very
much obliged to you for giving me that
information.

You certainly had a hand in the
forestry movement of the United States when
you typed practically all the National
Forest proclamations from 1891 to 1900.

What you say about the transfer of
the work to the field also interested me
greatly. Certainly, if anyone has a right
to be called an old-timer, you have.

With renewed and most hearty thanks,

Yours as always,

GP

chapter 2

Grover C. Blake
OREGON
1909-1931

*"One of the problems which faced Forest Officers in 1918
and 1919 was that in many cases, their income was not
sufficient to support themselves and families."*

—Grover C. Blake

There was no underestimating Pinchot's appreciation
for the narrative received by Oregon Ranger Grover C.
Blake as it contained just about everything the Old Chief asked
for. In his 25-page summary, Blake describes the sheep and
cattle wars in detail, the "dead lines" set by cattlemen to limit
wandering sheep, and the sheep mens' response. Blake takes us
on a journey through the "lush valleys" of the Deschutes, John
Day, and Crooked River describing how the range became
overstocked and deteriorated quickly.

Whether building trails, constructing fences, establishing
allotment lines, a ranger's work was physically challenging and
frequently filled with surprise. Blake shares an incident with
Pinchot in which he describes being out in the forest one day
when he discovered a horse in a most unusual situation. "We

were unable to visualize any condition where it would be possible for the animal to get himself in this place," Blake wrote. "Yet there he was, and we had no camera to prove our story." Chopping the smaller branch of the tree off at the ground, Blake liberated the horse who hobbled away, according to Blake, "without saying thank you."

Idleyld Park, Oregon

November 12, 1940.

Hon. Gifford Pinchot,

Washington D.C.

Dear Sir:

Your letter of December 11, 1939 to Supervisor
Vernon V. Harpham of Roseburg was shown to me by Mr.
Harpham a day or two ago with a request that I write
something of my early experiences as a contribution to
your very commendable efforts to preserve the history of
those early days of the Forest Service. Mr. Harpham fully
intends to supply his bit but, as yet, has not found the
time. I have often expressed the regret that someone of the
early Forest Service family had not taken steps to make
a permanent record of the experiences of the early days
while the Service was being founded and it is gratifying
indeed to know that you, my old chief and the father of the
Forest Service, have undertaken the job.

Naturally I want to be as helpful as possible but
before attempting to write of any of the events of my
early experiences I find myself facing several questions
which cause me to hesitate. First, there was nothing very
unusual about my experience. Just a duplication of the
experiences of, perhaps, dozens of others. The hardships,
handicaps, adverse public sentiment; the digging,
striving and persevering against odds to convert the

43

public and put into effect the new order of things was
the experience of all the personnel of that day. I entered
the service on May 4, 1909 and served continuously for 22
years. Before entering the Service I was employed for some
five years by eastern Oregon stockmen in handling sheep
and cattle on the ranges and during a portion of the range
war period.

In the second place, your letter bears a date of 11
months ago and I am wondering if anything I might be able
to contribute would not be too late for use in case it was
usable at all. In the third place, I am not blessed with
literary ability and I am afraid I would not be able to put
any of my early experiences into usable form. However, I
am more than interested in the undertaking and will be
glad to help if it is in my power. It is natural for we old
timers to reminisce and relive experiences of bygone days
and we are all anxious to have that part of the country's
history preserved.

It is a great privilege to have this opportunity to
contact you again after all these years and I hope to have
a reply from you, our old chief and the man who laid the
foundation for the conservation of our forest resources
and built the Forest Service.

Very truly yours,

G.C. Blake,

Idleyld Park, Oregon.

1615 Rhode Island Ave., N.W.,
Washington, D.C.,
November 18, 1940.

Mr. G.C. Blake,
Idleyld Park, Oregon.

Dear Mr. Blake:

Many thanks for yours of November
12, which has just reached me. You are by no
means too late, and I hope you will write up your
experiences in accordance with your letter.
Supervisor Harpham was exactly right in asking
you to do so. The fact that they were not unusual
is very far from being anything against them. What
I want above everything is not help for my book,
which, of course I deeply appreciate, but a record
of the early days of the Forest Service and of the
conditions which existed at that time; so I hope
you will send me your story.

With every good wish,

Faithfully yours,

GP

GP: AMB

Roseburg, Oregon

February 24, 1941.

Hon. Gifford Pinchot,

Washington, D.C.

Dear Sir:

Reference is made to your letter of November 18, 1940.

When I entered the Forest Service at Prineville, Oregon on May 4, 1909 the major activity in the Blue Mountains of Oregon was administration of grazing. My work for the next 15 years was in, what I have understood to be, the most intensely grazed section of the Deschutes National Forest and later the Ochoco.

I do not have the literary ability to properly describe conditions as they existed at that time nor the problems that faced the Forest Service. In order to show the enormity of these problems perhaps it would be better to go back some years and briefly review the history of grazing as it led up to the creation of the National Forests.

According to historical records the early settlers of Oregon filtered into the rich valleys to the west of the Cascade mountain range during the half century following the Lewis & Clark expedition. In the 1850s there were a few miners and trappers operating east of the Cascades but no agriculturists or home builders. One of the several reasons being that the Indians had almost complete control of the situation and it was quite a risk for white settlers to venture into that section. As the settlements became more populated in the Willamette and other valleys of Western Oregon some rather large herds of cattle were developed. In the 1870s these people began to look toward the grassy ranges of eastern Oregon and, as soldiers had been stationed along military road grants as a protection from Indians, a few herds were taken across the mountains to the great fields of grass lands to the east.

The lush valleys of the Deschutes, John Day, Crooked River and the famous Harney Valley were rapidly filled with cattle, sheep and horses. Before the turn of the century most of these ranges were controlled by large companys who had gained control of the range through possession of control spots, water holes etc. largely through fraud. Many instances are of record where employees were paid as low as $50 to file upon a tract of land under the homestead laws, secure patent and then deed it to the Company. For some years no effort was made to cut hay for winter feeding as the stock wintered nicely on the range but as time went on and the ranges became more crowded the size of a stockman's herd was governed by the amount of winter feed he could produce. The stock increased in numbers until even the summer feed was not sufficient to go around. Each summer the stock were moved farther and farther back into the Blue Mountains until the entire mountain area was covered by grazing sheep, cattle and horses during the summer months. The shade, cool mountain streams and the luscious peavine, lupines and many other weeds and grasses which covered the ground, made these forested areas a stockman's paradise.

The inevitable happened and the ranges became overstocked and began to deteriorate. Sheepmen would rush their flocks to the choice camps, crowding the receding snows in order to be first, trampling out the grass and other forage on the damp ground before they were large enough to provide feed. Thousands of cattle and hundreds of thousands of sheep were rushed into the Blue Mountains each spring.

Then came the range wars. Cattle do not do well on range grazed by sheep. So cattlemen began to establish "dead lines" against ranging sheep. Sheep crossing the "dead lines" were killed. Many sheep and a number of men were killed. The following letters will tend to illustrate the bitterness and boldness which had developed among the stockmen:

Prineville, Oregon,
June 17, 1904.

The Dalles Times Mountaineer

The Dalles, Oregon

"Conflicting range territory in Crook County led to the first open slaughter of sheep last Monday (June 13) where masked men shot and killed sixty-five head belonging to Allie Jones, a sheep owner residing about fifteen miles east of this city. The killing occurred on Mill Creek in the vicinity of the "dead lines" the men threatening a greater slaughter if the herds were not removed instantly from the district.***** The first outbreak in the sheep industry in this county recalls vividly the wanton slaughter which has recently occurred in Lake County, and marks the first steps in the range difficulties which are likely to be encountered during the coming season. The scene of the killing is in the

The open slaughter of sheep.
Photograph from the narrative of Clarence E. Favre (Served from 1910-1941)
in Idaho, Nevada, Wyoming, and R-4 Ogden, Utah.
Library of Congress. Manuscript Division.
Gifford Pinchot Collection. Old Timers Collection.

territory where an effort was made a short time ago to
establish lines for the sheep and cattle. Three weeks
ago the district was visited by a party of sheep owners
from Antelope and a meeting arranged between them and
the cattlemen in the southeastern part of the county.
The matter of ranging stock in the Blue Mountains was
gone over thoroughly, but a decision relative to the
establishment of limits failed to be reached. The sheep
men went home and the slaughter this week is a result of
their futile efforts to come to an understanding.

While it is not believed that open hostilities
will break out between sheep and cattle owners in this
territory during the summer ranging months, it is
asserted that an encroachment upon this disputed region
by nomadic sheep will be a signal for forcible resistance.

The "dead lines" of last year will be strictly enforced
which means that stockmen will not be occupying a
peaceable neighborhood."

"Sheep-Shooters' Headquarters,
Crook County, Oregon,
December 29, 1904.

Morning Oregonian,
        Portland, Oregon.
"Mr. Editor:
        Seeing that you are giving quite a bit of
publicity to the Sheep Shooters of Crook County, I thought
I would lend you some assistance by giving you a short
synopsis of the proceedings of the organization during
the past year. ——--—-Therefore if space will permit,
please publish the following report:

'Sheep Shooters' Headquarters, Crook County,
Oregon, December 29, 1904—Editor Oregonian: I am
authorized by the association (The Inland Sheep Shooters)
to notify the Oregonian to desist from publishing matter
derogatory to the reputation of sheep shooters of Eastern
Oregon. We claim to have the banner county of Oregon
on the progressive lines of sheepshooting, and it is my
pleasure to inform you that we have a little government
of our own in Crook County, and we would thank the
Oregonian and the Governor to attend strictly to their
business and not meddle with the settlement of the range
question in our province.
        We are the direct and effective means of
controlling the range in our jurisdiction. If we want
more range we simply fence it in and live up to the maxim
of the golden rule that possession represents nine points
of the law. If fencing is too expensive for the protection
of the range, dead lines are most effective substitutes
and readily manufactured. When sheepmen fail to observe

these peaceable obstructions we delegate a committee to
notify offenders, sometimes by putting notices on tent or
cabin and sometimes by publication in one of the leading
newspapers of the county as follows:

'You are hereby notified to move this camp
within twenty-four hours or take the consequences.
Signed, Committee.'

These mild and peaceful means are usually
effective, but in cases where they are not, our executive
committee takes the matter in hand, and being men of high
ideals as well as good shots by moonlight, they promptly
enforce the edicts of the association. ——Our annual
report shows that we have slaughtered between 8,000 and
10,000 head during the last shooting season and we expect
to increase this respectable showing during the next
season providing the sheep hold out and the Governor
and Oregonian observe the customary laws of neutrality.
————In some instances the woolgrowers of Eastern Oregon
have been so unwise as to offer rewards for the arrest
and conviction of sheep-shooters and for assaults on
herders. We have therefore warned them by publication
of the danger of such action, as it might result in our
organization having to proceed on the lines that 'Dead
men tell no tales.' This is not to be considered as a threat
to commit murder, as we do not justify such a thing except
where flock owners resort to unjustifiable means in
protecting their property.

(Signed) _____ Corresponding Secretary,
Crook County's Sheep Shooting Association of Eastern
Oregon."

It was at this period (May, 1904) that I came to
Eastern Oregon from the plains of Colorado where I grew
up on a cattle ranch. I was 20 years of age and went to work

on one of the larger ranches, that of the Prineville Land
and Livestock Co. During the next three years I worked for
several different stockmen and, as I grew older and more
experienced, my services became more and more in demand.
For the most part I worked for sheep men. By this time some
of the sheep men who were warring among themselves and
several herders killed by employees of rival sheep owners.
Most employees went about their work heavily armed.

All range wars were ended automatically when
the Forest Service administration went into effect and
the greatest war of all, which was impending at the time,
was averted.

In the fall of 1908 I was surprised to receive
a letter from the Civil Service Commission asking if I
would consider an appointment if replaced on the eligible
list. I replied that I would be in position to accept
appointment on the Deschutes Forest by May 1, 1909. Before
making reply I debated with myself for some time as I was
earning more money than the Forest Service offered but
my desire to get into the work over-ruled and on May 4,
1909 I reported to Supervisor Ireland at Prineville with
a saddle horse and packhorse and went to work as a Forest
Guard at $900 per year. In the years to come I worked
harder and longer hours than I ever had done before but I
was more interested in the work and enjoyed it more than
any I had ever done. I enjoyed the association of the finest
group of young men I had ever known and I never regretted
the move.

One of the problems which faced Forest
Officers in 1918 and 1919 was that in many cases, their
income was not sufficient to support themselves and

families. I remember that I paid as high as $28 for a
100-lb. sack of sugar and $55 each for two tires for my
car. Everything was in proportion. And my travels for the
wartime activities were done on my own expense. I just
could not make ends meet and I was really worried. Common
labor far exceeded our income but I knew that my patriotic
duty was to stay put. In fact I received a personal letter
to that effect from District Forester, George H. Cecil.
We got through somehow and Congress finally acted and
relieved the situation somewhat.

On July 3, 1920 I ran into a most unusual
incident. It was a wild, range horse lodged in a forked
tree. Virgil Allison, foreman for Elliott, Scoggins &
Wolfe, road contractors, and his wife were with me and
we were riding through the woods near the summit of the
mountain range on what was known as the Vowell Trail.
The tree forked at the ground level and opened to about
12 inches at breast height, holding the same slant on up
for a considerable distance. The horse was full grown and
weighed about 1100 lbs. His head, front feet and shoulders
were well through the forks on one side of the tree with
the front feet some four or five feet from the ground. His
hind feet were on the ground on the opposite side and his
body, just behind the shoulders wedged tightly between
the tree forks. He had evidently been in this position for
at least a day or two. He tried to fight us when we went
near his head. We were unable to visualize any condition
where it would be possible for the animal to get himself
in this place, yet there he was, and we had no camera to
prove our story. I chopped the smaller fork off near the
ground. It was about 16 inches in diameter. The skin and
flesh was badly worn from the horses sides due to his
struggling, and while he was in a bad way and very wobbly,
he was able to keep his feet and soon wobbled away without

saying thank you. This is one of many incidents of an unexplainable nature.

We were indeed grateful for the majority of the forest users who made every effort to comply with the Forest Service regulations. In those days there were no established headquarters for the ranger and no Government telephone lines and farmers lines were few and not dependable. The Supervisor had no way of quick communication with the ranger and seldom knew his whereabouts. There were no work plans and the job was the one which seemed most important from day to day. The ranger's headquarters were where his pack horse happened to be. I had a sort of homestead near my district which served as a sort of headquarters and where I kept a change of horses. I would take two horses into the field and by the end of two weeks they would be well rode down and fagged out so I would take them home and turn them out to pasture and start out with two fresh ones. This would give the sore backs a chance to heal also. The monthly reports were usually made out in the field with a pencil.

The outstanding event of 1917 for the Ochoco National Forest was the resignation of Homer Ross as Forest Supervisor. Mr. Ross had been responsible for much development during his term of service and we rangers were enjoying many conveniences we had not known when he came and the administration of our districts had been made much easier as a result of the improvements made.

Mr. Ross was replaced by Vernon V. Harpham who came to the Ochoco as Supervisor in the fall of 1917. Mr. Harpham's term of service has exceeded that of any

Ranger Ross's personal car adapted for use as fire engine.
Photo from the narrative of Homer B. Ross.
Library of Congress. Manuscript Division.
Gifford Pinchot Collection. Old Timers Collection.

other Supervisor of the Ochoco to date. His splendid personality, strict honesty and fairness in all his dealings made many friends for the Service. His personal interest in the well-being of his associates and the men who worked under him endeared him to all.

The hardest blow of my career came in October, 1917. Our little girl, now 4 years of age, took sick on September 28 with cholera infantum and passed away in Prineville on October 9.

Looking back on the problems of 32 years ago, noting the wonderful accomplishments of the Forest Service and the way it has grown up to date, is but to marvel. Somehow I like to reminisce on those days when we were striving to overcome the greatest handicaps of all, when I had the privilege of working as a member of such a splendid group of young men. The work was hard and the hardships plenty, but we were accomplishing things with our own hands and took great pride in it.

I hope someone will eventually write a story paying just tribute to the loyal women of the early Forest Service, who neglected their household duties to keep the wheels rolling, dispatching men to fires and attending to much of the Ranger's official work while their Ranger husbands were away on protracted field trips and their whereabouts unknown.

Very sincerely yours,

G. C. Blake,
Roseburg, Oregon.

Roseburg, Oregon

March 7, 1941.

Hon. Gifford Pinchot,

    Washington D.C.

Dear Sir:

    Reference is made to your letter of November 18, 1940.

    In a day or two I hope to have my story in the mail, but I am afraid the story is not well told and that it is more or less a failure as stories go. However, if I have been able to do you a service I will be more than happy about it. I feel deeply indebted to you for the kind and considerate treatment we, of the early Forest Service, enjoyed. It was you, my old chief, who created the Forest Service policy and thereby so influenced my life work. I am deeply grateful to you in many ways.

    Very truly yours,

        G.C.Blake,
        Roseburg, Oregon.

1615 Rhode Island Ave., N.W.
Washington D.C.,
March 12, 1941.

Mr. G.C. Blake,
Roseburg, Oregon.

Dear Blake:

      I am delighted to get your letter of
March 7, and especially appreciate what you
were good enough to say about the early days
of the Forest Service. Your story will be in
plenty of time, and I shall look forward to
it with the keenest interest.

      Yes, the old days were good days, and
I am mighty thankful to have had a hand in them.

      With all good wishes,

          Faithfully yours,

             GP

GP: AMB

1615 Rhode Island Ave., N.W.,
Washington, D.C.,
March 15, 1941.

Mr. G.C. Blake,
Roseburg, Oregon.

Dear Mr. Blake:

I hardly know how to thank you for
your most interesting letter of February 24,
which has just reached me, and which I have been
going over with the keenest interest. The stories
it contains of the early sheep and cattle wars in
Oregon are most valuable. And so are the anecdotes
of the tough times the Forest Service men had to
go through in the early days. I was particularly
delighted, also, with your comment on the
accomplishments of the Forest Service and your
tribute to the women of the Service. I agree with
you down to the ground.

With all good wishes,

Sincerely yours,

GP

GP:AMB

chapter 3

Robert L. Campbell
WASHINGTON D.C., CALIFORNIA, MONTANA, WASHINGTON STATE
1903-1919

"At about this time the "Use Book" was prepared, its very name indicating the changed departmental attitude toward the public domain, the "forest reserves," became National Forests, and a new official badge was adopted. I believe A.T. Allen designed the latter, or made valuable suggestions."

—Robert L. Campbell

*R*obert Campbell entered the Bureau of Forestry, the agency that preceded the Forest Service, by taking the Civil Service exam. Assigned to the Atlantic Building as a stenographer in 1903, Campbell attributed this "fortunate circumstance" to chance. The 11-page narrative he sent Pinchot describes how he made his way to the F Street office in Washington, D.C. to train with forest professionals such as Coert DuBois, Charles Shinn, Fritz Olmsted, and others. His position required he write with "meticulous care." That training changed his life. Campbell's narrative is filled with names, dates, and places that help us visualize the moment of transition as the conservation of forests, water, and land became a national priority.

In Campbell's narrative, the Atlantic Building is a beehive of activity as young stenographers type President Roosevelt's forest reserve land proclamations, draftsmen finish preparing their maps, while others create the "Use Book" describing the process and tools of conservation on the ground. Campbell reveals that it may have been F.E. "Fritz" Olmsted, one of the land examiners, who suggested the use of the expression "the greatest good for the greatest number" that appeared in many early agency documents. While Gifford Pinchot is credited with the expression, it is unlikely he cared whose idea it was. He was too busy keeping the agency moving forward.

In his narrative, Campbell reminds the old Chief of his qualities as a leader. "The Forester was a man marked by vigor and

Ranger Convention at the original Sierra Forest Headquarters,
Charles Howard Shinn residence, 1910.
Mr. Shinn is shown standing fourth from left.
From the narrative of Roy Boothe (Served in California 1907-1920).
Library of Congress. Manuscript Division.
Gifford Pinchot Collection. Old Timers Collection.

directness," he wrote. Pinchot could be terse, but his "straight forward manner, tempered with fairness," endeared him to his fellow workers. Through the recollections of Robert Campbell we meet foresters William L. Hall of Missouri, Charles Scott of Nebraska, Coert DuBois of New York, and Charles Shinn "surrounded by his books and papers, a constant source of inspiration" at Peace Cottage, his home in the Sierra foothills of California.

UNITED STATES DEPARTMENT OF AGRICULTURE
FOREST SERVICE
SIUSLAW NATIONAL FOREST

EUGENE, OREGON

January 9, 1940.

Mr. Gifford Pinchot,
1615 Rhode Island Ave. N.W.,
Washington, D.C.

Dear Mr. Pinchot:

I have your letter of December 11, and have written down a brief recollection narrative, which I am enclosing. I am afraid it will not be of very great value to your chief objective, as my work did not bring me much in contact to any great extent with the public sentiment of the times. However there might be something in it which will contribute to the whole.

I am glad to be of what assistance I can.

Very Sincerely,

Robert L. Campbell.

EARLY RECOLLECTIONS

I entered the Forest Service, then known as the Bureau of Forestry, on December 15, 1903. It was by chance. When my name reached the top of the Civil Service eligible list, it happened that the Bureau of Forestry needed a stenographer. I have always considered this a fortunate circumstance. Incidentally, at this time government positions were considered unattractive and killers of ambition and initiative.

Upon arriving in Washington, I found the Bureau occupying quarters in the Atlantic Bldg., on F Street, the office of Forester, Gifford Pinchot, being on the 7th floor. Wm. L. Hall was handling Forest Extension and giving advice to farmer and others as to tree planting etc., Thos. H. Sherrard was Chief of Forest Management, with parties of students in the field making work plans on private owned land: Geo. B. Sudworth was Dendrologist, Herman von Schrenk was in charge of Forest Products; Capt. Jas. B. Adams headed up operation and personnel.

The old Bureau of forestry had no public land to administer, its function being chiefly advisory, and my first job was to write, with meticulous care under the direction of Geo. G. Anderson, letters of transmittal for various government Publications.

This continued for several weeks until in the Spring of 1904, I was moved to the Section of Reserve Boundaries, whose Chief was F.E. Olmsted. Mr. Olmsted was in charge of a group of land examiners who were scouting the Western States to determine the suitability of forested regions for inclusion in forest reserves, as they were then called. As fast as maps and reports were received, they were put in shape and I typed very formal letters to "The Honorable, the Secretary of the Interior" for the signature of the Secretary of Agriculture recommending withdrawals from further entry pending decision as to establishment of a forest reserve by

"F. E. Fritz Olmsted. Always my good friend."
Photo from the narrative of H. J. Tompkins. Library of Congress. Manuscript Division.
Gifford Pinchot Collection. Old Timers Collection.

presidential proclamation. Among the examiners were
R.E. Benedict, R.V.R Reynolds, Coert DuBois, H.J. Tompkins,
W.H.B. Kent, John H. Hatton, E.T. Allen, Clyde Leavett.

Early in 1905, we moved up to the 7th floor.
Effective upon Feb. 1st of that year the administration of
the "forest reserves" was transferred from the Dept. of the
Interior to the Department of Agriculture and assigned to
the Bureau of Forestry, its name being changed to Forest
Service. Most of the land examiners became inspectors
and a thorough examination of field conditions began.
Under the former Forest Land office administration,
corruption and incompetency had been rampant. Dismissals
and suspension of members of the field force were made at
once, Supervisor Thomas at Los Angeles, was convicted of
misappropriation of funds. In some instances not only one

but a group of Rangers on a single reserve were suspended.
On the other hand, some of the more promising supervisors
were brought into Washington for training. L.F. Knipp was
one of these. The merit system was established. However
the problem of finding capable men was at this time rather
acute.

At about this time was written the letter from
Secretary Wilson to the Forester, found on page 3-A of
the old National Forest Manual, which contained the oft
repeated phrase "from the standpoint of the greatest good
for the greatest number". As I recall the incident, the
letter was really dictated by Mr. Olmsted, typed by myself
initialed by Mr. Pinchot, with his big bold "GP" and sent
over to the Secretary for signature.

At the time of the transfer of the reserves for the
Department of the Interior, Capt. J.B. Satterlee and M.P
Leland came over from the General Land Office, both of
whom continued to render faithful service. When writing
letters it was customary under General Land Office
procedure to brief the letter being answered before going
into the reply. In order to put a stop to this, Harry Hill,
who was then Mr. Pinchot's secretary, and I were asked to
prepare two letters, one showing the old style and the
other the form of composition to be thereafter used. We
spent some time on the sample letter written in the old
General Land Office Style, but after presenting it to the
Forester, Harry Hill reported by saying "Mr. Pinchot says
it is not rotten enough."

The Forester was a man marked by vigor and
directness of expression. I recall an instance of where
one of the field men, somewhat unfamiliar with office
procedure had written a rather factless letter to a
Congress man. It came back with the following dashed
across the face in the familiar hand of the Forester.
"Could not have been worse." In another instance, I recall
this choice bit of sarcasm, "I have written another reply
and I hope a better one." However it was this straight

forward manner, tempered with fairness, which endeared
Mr. Pinchot to his fellow workers.

At about this time the "Use book" was prepared, its
very name indicating the changed departmental attitude
toward the public domain, the "forest reserves," became
National Forests, and a new official badge was adopted. I
believe A.T. Allen designed the latter, or made valuable
suggestions.

At this junction, about the later fall of 1905, I
went on a six month furlough, from which I did not return
until about July 1906. Contrary to present restriction,
it was then possible to secure a furlough on no grounds
other than personal inclination so I satisfied a desire
to spend some time at home in this way. However, the
furlough roll became unduly large and it soon became
necessary to withdraw such liberality. During my absence
the reorganization of the field personnel had been going
on apace, and in October shortly after my return, I was
sent out to assist in the clerical work in the Leadville
National Forest and with headquarters at Leadville,
Colo. Jas. A. Blair was Acting Supervisor. At that time
E.N. Kavanagh, was a Forest Guard at Dillon, Colo. We had
a single office room, with store room attached in the
Post Office Building. Visitors were rare. There was no
office telephone. I recall making a recommendation that
the expense of one was not justified. We had an economy
complex in those days. A blanket of snow seemed to have
put a stop to forest activity. The beginning of technical
forestry as a part of management was now apparent. In the
office was Forest Assistant J.H. Ramskill, a recent forest
school graduate. A little later Mr. Blair was transferred
to the White River Forest and a new supervisor appeared
in the person of A.L. Shoup. He was interesting in that he
was a former druggist with little apparent knowledge of
forestry, or qualifications for the job. A Civil Service
examination, for the position of Forest Supervisor had

been held (it was only one.) and Mr. Shoup came from the
clerical list thus established. My stay in Leadville
was marked by one field trip. To make a timber sale
examination at about 11,000 ft. elevation.

Late in 1906, I was ordered to report at Harrison
Hot Springs, Calif., the headquarters of the Sierra (S)
Forest, where I found Coert Du Bois struggling with an
upset office. He had recently taken charge replacing
Harrison White, of Visalia. Jesse Brown was the District
Ranger. I recall that the night after I arrived DuBois
had called in one of the Rangers to inform him of his
suspension, but when the Ranger arrived he had a gun in
his belt, so DuBois decided to wait until a more opportune
time. However within a few days, Du Bois was ordered
to return to Washington, and W.B. Greeley arrived as
Forest Supervisor. This was one of the comparatively few

"Sierra Forest Ellis Meadow. Mr. and Mrs. Chas H. Shinn,
Ruth Shinn, Mr. Tyler, Audie Wofford, H.J. Tompkins."
From the narrative of H.J. Tompkins. Library of Congress. Manuscript Division.
Gifford Pinchot Collection. Old Timers Collection.

instances at that time when Eastern College graduates
were placed in charge of National Forests. However,
Greeley was a resident of California, his father being
a clergyman in Oakland. Harrison Hot Springs was 40
miles from the nearest railroad, and illustrated the
old practice of General Land office days of locating the
headquarters in the town which best met the convenience
of the Supervisor whoever that happened to be. Shortly
after my arrival Russell G. Pond came as Technical
Assistant. At that time the national forests were still
pretty much "reserves" in a literal sense and were not
much used. Presently Greeley mounted his horse and went
for a long trip to the East of the Sierras, while Pond and
I worked over what few records there were, and kept the
office open. Later in the fall I spent several weeks in
Visalia, securing statistic data at the local land office.
The holidays were spent with Greeley and his parents in
Oakland.

Early in 1907, I moved up to Northfork, the
headquarters of the Sierra (N) Forest, at that time in
charge of Chas. Howard Shinn. Mr. Shinn lived in "Peace
Cottage" on Malam Ridge in the foot hills of the Sierras,
surrounded by his books and papers, a constant source
of inspiration to all who came in contact with him and
one of the real pioneers of conservation. A quiet winter
followed. Forest activities were largely confined to
timber sales, special uses and claims cases. It was not
yet a year round job, with its multiplicity of reports and
comprehensive social and economic aspects, as at present,
and improvement work as we have come to know it had
not yet begun. Aside from an excursion to mark a 40 Acre
timber tract and a special use application examination. I
recall no field activity, although the roll call of forest
offices at headquarters was a long one. "Boot" Taylor,
Gene Tully, Andie Wofford, Conrad Alles, Bill Throwler,
Edw. Bartlett and Geo. Caven. H.J. Tompkins came out as

a technical assistant, accompanied by Mrs. Tompkins, a recent bride, for whom a cabin was built and properly showered with tin ware. Northfork was also 40 miles from the railroad, by an all day stage, and visitors were few.

The idealism of Mr. Shinn, however made up for any lack of forest activity. I can yet hear his merry shout, "Wake up sleep heads," as he would pass our cabin in the darkness of 4 o'clock A.M. going down to Northfork to take the stage to the valley.

In the early spring of 1907, I returned to Washington. By that time the new field organization was taking shape, and the beginning of our present intensive system of personnel training began to appear. Supervisors were brought into Washington in groups of six, for 3 month detail, one for each of the six inspection districts. These inspection districts were the forerunner of the present regional system. A "Bull pen", as it was called was established, in which work now handled by the Division of Operation was carried on, of which I took charge. Many of the Supervisors had never been East before, few of them had much experience in office work, and while efficiency may have suffered, training results should have been great for men started from scratch.

I pass them in review: G.F. Allen, Geo W. Melham, Gilbert Coleman, R.L.P. Bigelow, H.A.E. Marshall, F.C.W. Pooler, S.C. Bartrun, W.M. Slosson, Ross McMullan, W.H. Goddard, Zeph Jones, H.W. Thurston and many others.

This was the time of the crisis with Japan over the school situation in California. Suddenly Supervisor H.W. Thurston, of one of the forests near Yellowstone National Park, and who was closely related by marriage to W.F. Cody (Buffalo Bill), was taken out of the bull pen and sent West on a secret mission. Rumor had it that he was assisting in reconnoitering mountain passes as a military precaution, but I never learned just what was the purpose of the trip.

Birthday card from Joseph M. Cuenin to Gifford Pinchot.
Cuenin served in Colorado from 1905-1934.
Library of Congress. Manuscript Division.
Gifford Pinchot Collection. Old Timers Collection.

Eventually, the activity of a small group of Western Senators caused Congress to take from President Roosevelt, the authority to create National Forests by proclamation. The weeks preceding that date were busy ones. Maps were rapidly prepared, reports gotten in shape so that before relinquishing his authority, the President was able to proclaim a large number of new forests.

The "Bull Pen" continued to function and about July 1, 1908, when I turned it over to N.L. Downs, signed out on the travel register, and left for a field trip, which took me out of Washington for good.

While on the trip I encountered many of the early service personnel. Each office had a single clerk and my work consisted in checking over the files, the few accounts, records then in use, office arrangements, case records, training the clerks in office methods,

and assisting the Supervisor where possible. I made no
reports, stayed as long as conditions required, prepared
my own itinerary, and was pretty much of a free lance, my
most vital connection with the Washington office being
the monthly salary and expense check. I might recall
some of the names and places. A short trip into Wyoming
out of Denver extended the grand Encampment, where Jas.
R. Blackhall was in charge. Down at Saratoga, Wyo. Wm. N.
Pearce was the Supervisor. He was out but F.G. Agee was in
charge at the time. There was an office at Ft. Collins, Colo.
Several days were spent at Glenwood Springs where Harry
H. French was in charge at the time of my visit R.P. Imes
was there on timber Sale work. I did not find Supervisor
Dr. H.K. Parker in on my arrival at Delta. Farther on at
Garrison was found Wm. R. Krentzer, one of the earliest
defenders of the need for conservation, whose Assistant
at the time was a man by the name of Berkley. At Monte
Vista, Dr. F. C. Spencer was on the firing line. A stage
trip of 40 miles, or so took me to Sewache, where I recall
another early forestry pioneer, Joe Cuenin. Upon moving
on Westward and arrival at Salt Lake City, I encountered
Clyde Leavitt, who had been sent out from Washington to
arrange for the establishment of a District office. (By
this time the plan of decentralizing and bringing the
administration close to the people had been determined
upon.) Leavitt and I visited the Salt Lake City Chamber of
Commerce, on this quest, and later went over to Ogden and
dined with one Kiesel, who later built for the Service the
building in Ogden it eventually occupied.

Upon moving on Westward and arrival at Salt Lake
City, I encountered Clyde Leavitt, who had been sent out
from Washington to arrange for the establishment of a
District office. (By this time the plan of decentralizing
and bringing the administration close to the people had
been determined upon.) Leavitt and I visited the Salt

Lake City Chamber of Commerce, on this quest, and later
went over to Ogden and dined with one Kiesel, who later
built for the Service the building in Ogden it eventually
occupied.

Enroute to the Pacific Coast, I stopped at Boise,
where I met Supervisor Emil Granjean, who I remember was
at that particular time concerned about the attitude of
Senator Borah. Over at Emmet, Idaho, Carl Arentsen was
acting in charge, the return trip across the Northern part
of the country took me to Wallace, where W.C. Weigle had
recently assumed charge. Don Skeels was there also, who
later became connected with the University of Montana.
At Kalispell, I met one of the older Supervisors in the
person of I.N. Haines. Page S. Bunker, later to become
State Forester of Alabama, I believe, was in charge of
the other forest with headquarters at Kalispell. After
a stage trip into Chateau, I found there W.B. Greeley,
who was soon to become District Forester in District 1,
and together we interviewed W.H. Dangs then in charge.
V. Gifford Lantry was down at Livingston, and J.B.
Seely at Sheridan, C.C.Hall was Supervisor at Anaconda,
Supervisor Shoonover was at {Lib} by, also Glen Smith, as
his Assistant. Smith was doing land examination work
at the time and was not always welcome in the days when
fictitious claims were common. I recall him telling me of
a case where a small boy who recognized him, did not wait
for him to approach the house, but rushed out shouting
"Father ain't home". I am depending on memory for these
names and places. My work did not bring me in very much
contact with forest users as visitors to the offices were
few in those days, but as I now recall sentiment was most
adverse in Colorado, Idaho and Montana following in the
order named.

It had now been decided to decentralize the
Service and establish Regional offices. What was done
effective January 1, 1909. As a result I became Chief of
Maintenance at Missoula, and terminated my trip there.

At the start these district offices were over-
manned and the original plan of having a Chief and
Assistant chief for each branch was dropped. It is
interesting to note that as organized the Missoula office
contained three men destined to be Chiefs of the Forest
Service: i.e., District Forester Wm. B. Greeley, Assistant
Dist. Forester F.A. Silcox, and Robert Y Stuart, A.W. Cooper
was Chief of Silviculture, and David T. Mason as Assistant
Chief; Richard H. Rutlidge Chief of Operation and R.T.
Stuart as Assistant Chief; C.H. Adams Chief of Grazing
and Wellman Holbrook as Assistant Chief; J.P. Marten
District Engineer and E.W. Cramer his assistant. Later
Cooper resigned and Stuart was moved over into the vacant
position. We had a law officer named Aiken, who went on a
woods excursion with a draftsman named Tripp, became lost
and was reported as having shot himself. My duties were
light. We had no warehouse. Field property accounting was
still centralized in Washington.

At this time H.I. Loving was District Fiscal Agent,
with John A. Urbanowitz as Assistant. The latter who by
that time had become Fiscal Agent later was convicted of
defalcation of a large sum, this being the only serious
offence of the kind that I recall in more than 30 years of
Forest Service experience.

In the year 1909, at the request of Mr. Silcox, I
made a quiet visit to Land offices in Lewiston, Ida. and
Montana points in search of information as to whether
any private filings had been made on former power site
withdrawals. This was during the controversy which
revolved around the Cunningham Claims, in Alaska, and
divergent policies of the Interior and Agriculture
Departments, and which finally resulted in the retirement
of Mr. Pinchot. It appeared that a large number of power
site withdrawals had been revoked by the Department of
the Interior, and it was desired to learn whether or not

any filings by private parties had quickly followed. I prepared township plats showing my findings but do not recall that there were any such filings had been made.

Early in 1910 a desire to live on the Pacific Coast led me to request a transfer and I was assigned as Chief Clerk (and only clerk) on the Washington Forest (now Mt. Baker) with headquarters at Bellingham, Wash., where I arrived Feb. 12, 1910.

At that time the struggle to establish the correctness of the conservation policies of the Forest Service was about over as far as Northwest Washington was concerned. There was scant opposition, and this limited to a small section of the lumbering and private interests. Upon arrival I found Chas. H. Park, as Supervisor and F.H. Brundage as Forest Assistant. The old Washington Forest contained about 1,500,000 Acres and was practically uninhabited. Scarcity of natural feed made use of horses inconvenient, and the "hike" of 45 miles into the Upper Skagit River Country, a like distance to the mineralized region at the summit of the Cascade required a couple of days. The first telephone line was built in 1909. All out side activity ceased during the winter months, and there was then some point to the often repeated question, "What do you do in the winter time?" During the years proceeding and during the World War, covering the period of 1910-1919, there were few changes and the range of forest activities increased rather slowly, although steadily.

My latter assignments were on the Umpqua, Deschute and Siuslaw Forests, in Oregon, my present position being Administrative Assistant on the last named Forest, with headquarters at Eugene, Oregon.

Robert L. Campbell.

1615 Rhode Island Ave. N.W.,
Washington D.C.,
January 31, 1940.

Mr. Robert L. Campbell,
Forest Supervisor,
Siuslaw National Forest,
Eugene, Oregon.

Dear Campbell:

My best thanks for yours of
January 9 which would have been answered
long ago except for the flu. I am de-
delighted to get your material, for there is
much in it that will be of real use. I
am particularly glad of what you have
written about North Fork and Charlie
Shinn.

With every good wish and great
appreciation,

Yours as always,

GP

GP:AMB

Gifford Pinchot. Pennsylvania Avenue, Washington, D.C. March 4, 1925.

chapter 4

Clarence E. Dunston

South Carolina, Indiana, Idaho, Washington, Region 4 (Ogden), Nevada, Michigan, Washington D.C., 10th Engineers, California, and Region 5 (San Francisco)
1904–1940

"I am sure that every one of us young Forest Assistants started out to his field post, after that brief inspirational training course, fired with the determination to do his utmost to forward the cause of conservation in the United States."

—Clarence E. Dunston

We learn from Clarence Dunston's narrative that his career in forestry was inspired by his aunt, Helen Louise Dunston, who kept herself abreast of what her nephew referred to as "forward-thinking National movements." Dunston served in at least eleven different posts with the U.S. Forest Service between the years 1904 and 1940.

Dunston first served in the South and Midwest consulting with private landowners to develop landscape and forestry plans in order to "arouse the interest of timberland owners in sustained yield forestry management." While these early attempts were not, according to Dunston, always brilliantly executed, they formed the foundation upon which forestry was practiced in the Southern United States.

From its inception, the U.S. Forest Service has performed heroic deeds with limited resources and intermittent support. It is the humble, frequently-criticized agency whose task few understand, but which is, in fact, herculean: to maintain the forest while mediating between competing forces on an increasingly depleted land base. Today, having developed a greater understanding of local, regional, and planetary challenges to the maintenance of integrated and sustainable landscapes, ecosystems, and wildlife, we might consider how the Old Timer narratives serve as a resource, as Pinchot predicted, "of almost unbelievable historical value." They point to the Agency's inviolable commitment to the conservation of natural resources and the foundation of democracy and public well-being.

C.E. Dunston's narrative provides a keyhole through which to view today's challenges including sustainable harvesting and forest health. While many constituents and western communities regard the U.S. Forest Service as de facto firefighters and adjacent forests as public parks, land management agencies are charged with ever-increasing responsibility for forest health, including water, wildlife, and native species conservation.

UNITED STATES DEPARTMENT OF AGRICULTURE
FOREST SERVICE
CALIFORNIA REGION

760 Market St.
San Francisco, California

February 23, 1940

Hon. Gifford Pinchot,
1615 Rhode Island Ave. N.W.,
Washington D.C.

Dear Mr. Pinchot:

In response to your good letter of December 11, 1939, I am enclosing a rather general account of my official activities from 1905 to the present. Since my early official diaries are widely scattered, I have had to rely upon my memory and, therefore, it is possible that some minor mistakes may have been made in my narrative.

Very sincerely yours,

C.E. Dunston

San Francisco, Calif,
February 19, 1940.

THE PERSONAL NARRATIVE

OF

CLARENCE E. DUNSTON

The inspiration to make forestry my life work was given me by my Aunt Helen Louise Dunston, a teacher in the Buffalo State Normal School. I presume her interest in forestry was developed through wide reading and active participation in most forward-looking National movements. My entire high school course in Buffalo was directed toward entering the Forest School at Cornell University. It was a very keen disappointment to learn that Governor Odell had failed to approve the appropriation item for the continuance of the forestry course at Cornell in the year 1904 when I graduated from high school. After much reading of curricula of the Yale, Michigan, and Biltmore forestry courses, it was decided, in family conference, that I should enter the Biltmore Forest School in September 1904.

I have always felt fortunate in having studied under such brilliant and inspirational teachers as Dr. Carl A. Schenck and Dr. Clifton D. Howe. Biltmore was unique among the technical forestry schools of the country in that the entire course was conducted in a great forest laboratory, the George W. Vanderbilt Estate of over 100,000 acres, in the Appalachian Mountains. In a space of from 12 to 14 months (no vacations) classroom and field instruction was given in all the main branches of the science and art of forestry.

My first contact with an official of the Forest Service was in the special course on forest working plans given at Biltmore by J. Girvin Peters in the fall of 1905.

He aroused my interest in that activity to such an extent
that I wrote the Service at Washington applying for a
job as Forest Student on one of the working plan's field
parties. When a reply came from Associate Chief Forester
Overton W. Price offering me a job in A.E. Braniff's
working plan party on the Burton Lumber Company tract
near Charleston, South Carolina, I lost no time in
accepting in spite of the fact that I had just received an
offer of a forestry position from the Cleveland Cliffs Iron
Company in the Northern Peninsula of Michigan.

I reported for duty to Braniff about November 15,
1905, at this camp near Monks Corners, South Carolina.
A few days later Braniff left for Washington to assume
more important duties and Forest Assistant Merrill
replaced him as Chief of Party. This job for the Burton
Lumber Company was one of many similar projects, the
chief purpose of which, from the standpoint of the Forest
Service, was to arouse the interest of timberland owners
in sustained yield forestry management. While our
early attempts in this line were not always brilliantly
executed, I have no doubt that they formed a substantial
part of the foundation upon which present forestry
practices in the Southern States are based.

Upon completion of field work on the Burton
tract in late February 1906, I returned to my home in
Buffalo, New York, to prepare for the U.S. Civil Service
examination for the position of Forest Assistant. I shall
always remember the date of that examination—April 18—
because when I handed my completed papers to the examiner
he showed me the headlines of the evening newspaper,
telling of the destruction of San Francisco by earthquake
and fire. Later I.F. (Eli) Eldredge, one of my Biltmore
classmates, recounted to me, in his inimitable manner,
his experiences in San Francisco on that memorable date
when he, too, had intended to take the Forest Assistant
examination.

In May 1906, I received a letter from the Forest
Service restoring me to duty as Forest Student and
assigning me to the examination of farm woodlots
in Indiana with the purpose of advising owners on
silvicultural practices designed to yield the most
favorable economic results. I reported to S.J. Record at
Wabash College, Crawfordsville, Indiana, who as I recall
it, then held a Forest Service appointment as Extension
Forester in Indiana at a nominal salary and at the same
time was employed at the College to give courses in
botany and forestry subjects. Under Record's guidance and
general supervision I spent the next few months touring
Indiana, examining woodlots, doing my best to explain
the advantages of sane woods practices to farm owners,
writing reports descriptive of woodlots visited, and
embodying my recommendations as to cultural treatment.

Late in June 1906, while still in Crawfordsville,
I received a letter signed by Overton W. Price informing
me that I had passed the Forest Assistant examination and
would shortly receive a permanent appointment in the
Forest Service. I was instructed to report in Washington
early in July for a brief detail prior to being assigned to
one of the National Forests.

As I recall it, there were about twenty in the
group of new Forest Assistants assembled in the Atlantic
Building for an intensive course in Forest Service
objectives, policies, and procedures. The spirit of youth
pervaded the Atlantic Building at that time. Our Chief,
Gifford Pinchot, was still a young man. Several men
holding imposing titles as Division Chiefs were in their
middle twenties. I am sure that every one of us young
Forest Assistants started out to his field post, after
that brief inspirational training course, fired with the
determination to do his utmost to forward the cause of
conservation in the United States.

I was very happy over being assigned to the
Sawtooth and Payette National Forests, then in charge

of Forest Supervisor Frank A. Fenn, with headquarters
in Boise, Idaho. I reached Boise about July 15, 1906, and
immediately reported to Major Fenn in his modest office
over the principal hardware store of the City. Senator
William E. Borah had his law office in the same building.
Major Fenn received me with the utmost courtesy and
quickly made me feel thoroughly at home as a member of
his official family. His clerk, Wickersham, a six-foot
ex-cowpuncher, and one or two of his rangers were in the
office at the time. After a pleasant general discussion
of Forest Service matters, Major Fenn began to outline
his plans for my work. I was to spend the remainder of the
summer in the high Sawtooth range with headquarters at
the small mining town of Atlanta on the headwaters of the
Boise River. It would be necessary that I supply myself
with a saddle horse and a pack horse, together with riding
and camp equipment. A good saddle horse could be bought
for $100 and a pack horse for $50. Subsistence for myself
and my two horses would cost an average of $3.50 a day. My
per diem allowance of $1.25 would defray this expense in
part.

I have never been a good poker player, and I suppose
Major Fenn detected a somewhat anxious expression as I
searched vainly in my mind for a way to meet this initial
investment. Quietly he asked me to step into the hall with
him. There, after telling me he appreciated the fact that
most young men recently out of school were not apt to be
well supplied with cash, he inquired very courteously as
to the state of my finances. With equal frankness, I replied
that I had a total of about $10 in my pocket. Thereupon
the good Major told me he had decided it would be a much
better plan to send me to assist Carl Imes, District Ranger
of the Cottonwood District near Boise, on some important
timber sales work. I would need only a saddle horse, and he
was sure that a suitable animal should be bought for about
$35. He had an old saddle and bridle in the storeroom that
would serve my purpose. I could board at Ranger Imes' home

at moderate cost. As to the immediate financing of these
necessary items, that could be arranged quite readily
through a small loan at the bank. Within a few hours all
these details had been attended to, and I was the proud
owner of a buckskin pony. A few days later I rode up to Carl
Imes' cabin on Cottonwood Creek and reported for duty.
Carl, by the way, was a brother of Richard Imes who at that
time was Forest Supervisor of the Black Hills National
Forest in South Dakota, and who later was Assistant
District Forester in charge of Operation, Region 4 at
Ogden, Utah. I found plenty of work to keep me busy in
helping Carl with timber marking and log scaling on
several small sawtimber sales. My training at Biltmore in
this line, although mostly in hardwood types and under
quite different logging conditions, proved very helpful
to me. Carl was grateful for this assistance and soon
turned over to me most of his timber sales field work.

Late in the summer or early fall of 1906, Major Fenn
decided to send me to a new large timber sale on Clear
Creek, a tributary of the South Fork of the Payette River
some forty miles northeast of the old mining settlement
Idaho City. While in Boise making preparations for
the trip to this new assignment, I met Emil (Charley)
Grandjean, then an Assistant Ranger whom Major Fenn
had decided to send with me to this large new sale to the
Idaho White Pine Milling Company. Charley Grandjean
was one of the most colorful of all the early rangers
in the Forest Service. Of well-to-do, cultured Danish
parentage, Charley had sought adventure in the New World,
coming almost directly from Denmark to Idaho at the
age of eighteen. He was a born naturalist and woodsman
and thus quite readily took to trapping in the Rockies,
both as a means of livelihood and because of his deep
love for the primitive life in the mountains. Soon his
reputation as the most skillful and successful trapper
in the Sawtooth Range spread far and wide. Unlike most
trappers and woodsmen, Charley never became uncouth

either in personal appearance or manner. He was known
as the "Gentleman Trapper." During his occasional visits
to Boise, or other settlements, he always dressed in
excellent taste and might well be taken to be a successful
business or professional man. Charley and I soon became
warm friends. Much to our amusement we were frequently
taken to be father and son. Charley was then thirty-eight
and I was twenty-one.

While in Boise at the time, Charley Grandjean
and I attended a number of court sessions of the famous
Mayer, Heywood and Pettibone trial for the murder of
Governor Steunnenberg. Rarely in American criminal
court annals has there been a more dramatic legal battle.
It was thrilling to see and hear such brilliant attorneys
as Clarence Darrow for the defense and William E. Borah
for the prosecution. On one memorable afternoon, two
distinguished guests sat side by side near the Judge and
during intervals in the trial chatted as though they were
old friends. They were Chief Forester Gifford Pinchot and
the brilliant young dramatic star, Ethel Barrymore, who
was then appearing in Boise in "Captain Jinks."

Ranger Grandjean and I found we were breaking
new ground in starting the administration of this large
timber sale on Clear Creek. Although it comprised only
a few million board feet of ponderosa and Douglas fir
timber, we were told it was the largest sawtimber sale
thus far approved in any of the National Forests. The
preliminary negotiations with the officials of the Idaho
White Pine Milling Company as well as the sale appraisal
had been handled by C.S. Chapman, Inspector of the
Washington Office. Chapman spent a few days on the sale
area with Charley and me, showing us the sale boundaries,
discussing contract conditions and giving us his ideas
about timber marking. He impressed upon us the necessity
for doing our utmost to satisfy the purchasers to come
out successfully with this new venture. As I look back

now, I wonder how any sane businessman could convince
themselves that they had a reasonable chance to make a
success of that undertaking. The company erected a costly
sawmill at Nampa, Idaho on the Oregon Short Line branch of
the Union Pacific Railroad. Log transportation involved
driving about five miles of Clear Creek to its junction
with the South Fork of the Fayette River and fifty or sixty
miles of that turbulent stream to Emmett, Idaho. There the
logs were to be impounded by shear boom and loaded on flat
cars for rail haul to Nampa.

Silvicultural marking rules had not as yet been
developed for our guidance but, after brief instruction
from Inspector Chapman, Charley and I began blazing and
placing the U.S. stamp on a heavy proportion of the large
yellow pines in the initial logging unit near camp. While
I did endeavor to put into practice the silvicultural
precepts learned at the Forest School, I fear I was unduly
influenced by the purchaser's need to obtain a heavy cut
in order that his venture might prove to be successful.

Never before or since that time have I seen such
an aggregation of skilled, devil-may-care lumberjacks.
They were chiefly recruited from lumber camps of Maine
and the Lake States and, for the most part, were of French-
Canadian and Irish extraction. Joe Bodin, Pat Shanahan,
"Blackie" (I never learned his last name) stand out in my
memory as the most skillful axmen and cant-hook men I
have ever known. The camp boss, Mr. Henry, was a kindly,
rugged giant then in his fifties. Both bunk house and cook
house were made of logs with the chinks well daubed with
mud and the roofs covered deeply with earth to insure
warmth within during the long cold winter. Charley, with
my rather awkward assistance, made a similar small log
cabin for our home and headquarters. Then we laid in our
winter's supply of canned goods, dried fruit, flour, beans,
and cured meat. When freezing weather came, Charley shot
a buck and suspended it from a limb well out of reach of
coyotes and other wild animals.

During a lull in our work, when we were well ahead with the timber marking, we decided to make a scouting trip on horseback to examine some good patches of timber up the South Fork of the Payette which Charley recalled having seen in previous pack-horse trips. Upon our return to the logging camp several days later we learned, to our keen disappointment, that during our absence Chief Forester Pinchot and Supervisor Fenn had paid an inspection visit to our camp in the course of a long buckboard trip on the Sawtooth and Payette Forests. In a brief, kindly but firmly worded note we were informed that our timber marking was considerably too heavy, and we were instructed to go over all marked, uncut portions of the sale area and cross out with blue keel crayon thrifty marked trees that should be kept for a future crop. This proved to be an excellent lesson for us, and Charley and I worked diligently and faithfully to correct our mistake.

Early the following spring, preparations were made for the log drive down Clear Creek and the Payette River. Three bateaux, each large enough to carry several men, were constructed and given preliminary trials in the Payette near the mouth of Clear Creek. It proved to to be an Herculean task to drive the logs down the boulder-strewn five-mile stretch of Clear Creek, but the small crew of experienced "river hogs" accomplished the job with no major casualties. Then began the long perilous drive down the Payette through rocky gorges and long stretches of "white water."

Tragedy struck this little band of river drivers with lightning speed one morning when the main drive was nearing Garden Valley some thirty miles below Clear Creek. One of the bateaux bearing the boss of the drive, a sturdy Irishman, had gone ahead through a deep gorge beyond which it was known there was a stretch of turbulent rapids. Bosses of the crew in the other boats were instructed to wait an hour or two before following so

that in case of any accident to the first boat word could
be returned to the waiting crew before they continued
down stream.

In the absence of news from the first boat, it was
finally decided safe for the others to proceed. As the first
of these following boats rounded the bend below the gorge,
its occupants learned why no messenger had returned from
the pilot bateau which was then lying overturned and
lodged between huge boulders. A similar fate awaited the
on-coming boat crews. Only about half the men in these
three boats survived that terrible experience.

That was, so far as I know, both the first and the
last big log drive on the South Fork of the Payette. Only
a fraction of the logs that had started the drive finally
reached the boom at Emmett, and they were so badly broken
and battered as to be scarcely worth taking to the mill.
Shortly thereafter, the Idaho White Pine Milling Company
failed and thus ended the first big logging operation on
Clear Creek.

Just before Christmas 1906. Major Fenn called
both Ranger Grandjean and myself into Boise. Logging
operations on the big sale had been shut down due to
deep snow. At about that time notice was received from
Washington of a major realignment of boundaries of the
Sawooth and Payette Forests and the establishment of
separate jurisdictions for each of these Forests.

At about the same time this news of National Forest
administrative changes reached the public through local
press the smoldering fire of resentment, among both
sheepmen and cattlemen, against what they considered
to be unjust Governmental restrictions on the use of the
public ranges, flared up throughout Central and Southern
Idaho. Major Fenn, thoroughly schooled in politics and
who had served at least one term as Speaker of the House
in the Idaho State Legislature, did his utmost through
addressing stockmen's meetings and in office conferences

Ranger Franklin Reed, Coast of Washington Near Quenalt River.
From the narrative of H. J. Tompkins. Library of Congress. Manuscript Division.
Gifford Pinchot Collection. Old Timers Collection.

with leaders of the industry, to bring about a change of
sentiment in this respect.

All his rangers were pressed into service, each
to do his bit in his District in an effort to win over the
stockmen to a less belligerent attitude toward the Forest
Service. Even the young, greenhorn Forest Assistant so
recently arrived from the East was sent to Hailey in the
Sawtooth Range to explain to a large group of stockmen
the purpose and application of the grazing regulations as
contained in the Use Book.

During the summer and early fall of 1907, under
Supervisor Grandjean's instructions, I visited each
district of the Forest working with the rangers largely
in the capacity of an instructor in an effort to improve
timber sale administration. During that summer also,
I spent some time in the field with various inspectors
from the Washington office, among whom were C.S.Chapman,
Franklin W. Reed, and L.L. White. Doubtless, I expressed
to these inspectors my great interest in timber sales
work and also ventured the hope that I might eventually
be transferred to a field position in the Washington

Office of Silviculture. In November 1907 that hope was
realized when I received instructions through Supervisor
Grandjean to report to Washington for permanent
reassignment in the Branch of Timber Sales.

The winter of 1907-1908 stands out in my
memory as one of the happiest and most interesting of
my life. It was a thrilling experience to be closely
associated with such men as W.B. Greeley, E.E. Carter,
and Earl Clap in Forest Management and to rub shoulders
with leaders in other offices of the Service, including
A.F. Potter, L.F. Kneipp. George B. Sudworth, W.L. Hall,
and Raphael Zon. Always we were conscious of the strong,
kindly, able leadership of our Chief Gifford Pinchot.
The training received that winter in report and letter
writing and in office administration has proved to be of
lasting benefit throughout my career.

In the winter of 1909-10, the press of
Washington and throughout the country was filled with
accounts of disclosures by Special Agent Louis R. Glavis,
of the General Land Office, in regard to Alaska coal land
frauds and of growing tension between the Department of
Agriculture and the Department of the Interior in that
respect. Soon this became known as the Pinchot-Ballinger
controversy.

While most of us in the Washington office
realized from newspaper accounts that the breaking point
would be reached eventually, I am sure nearly everyone
was shocked and astounded one day in January or early
February, 1910, when early extra editions of the papers
announced the dismissal by President Taft of the Chief
Forester Pinchot, Associate Forester Price, and one or two
others high in authority in the Forest Service. A spirit
of gloom and confusion pervaded the Atlantic Building
on that memorable morning. Shortly after the lunch hour,
word was passed around the various offices that Mr.
Pinchot wished us all to assemble in the large meeting
room on the 8th floor. It was strictly a Forest Service

gathering. No member of the press was admitted and no stenographic report of Mr. Pinchot's talk was made. In my mind's eye, I can still see our Chief as he entered the room with long quick strides, characteristically erect and smiling. He talked to us fully an hour and not once did he mention the dramatic events which had preceded this meeting. Not a single word of bitterness or rancor was spoken. Instead we were urged to carry on the good fight for the conservation of the Nation's forests and other natural resources with the same energy and enthusiasm that had always characterized our organization. I think we all realized that Mr. Pinchot regarded his release from official duties as giving him greater opportunity than previously to advance the cause of conservation.

In early May 1917, while on the Flathead Indian Reservation in Montana, I received a telegram from William B. Greeley, Chief of Silviculture, U.S. Forest Service, offering me a commission as First Lieutenant in the 10th Engineers (Forestry) which was then being organized. Two months later I was ordered to report to the officers' training camp at American University, Washington, D.C. My training period was cut short when I received orders to leave for France with a small group of officers under the command of Major Greeley (later Lt. Colonel). There were twelve in that group who sailed with the Second Engineers, a regular army regiment, on the S.S. Finland from Hoboken, New Jersey, August 7, 1917. We landed in Saint Nazaire, France, August 20, and on the following day our small party reached Paris, where we were greeted by Major Henry S. Graves who had been making advance preparation for several weeks with French authorities for operations by the 10th Engineers. I shall always regard the twenty-two months spent in France as one of the most interesting and useful periods of my life. I returned to the United States late in April 1919, with the rank of Captain and received my discharge from the Army May 16.

William B. Greeley, (1879-1955). Third Chief of the U.S. Forest Service.
Photo from the narrative of Frances Cuttle. Library of Congress. Manuscript Division.
Gifford Pinchot Collection. Old Timers Collection.

While in Washington at that time, I called upon Chief Forester Graves and, to my surprise and pleasure, I learned I was slated for a Forest Supervisor position in either Montana or California. My old friend, Colonel Coert Dubois, District Forester of the California District, who chanced to be in Washington on official business, promptly arranged for my appointment as Supervisor of the Lassen National Forest, and a few weeks later I arrived at Mineral, California, the Forest headquarters, to take charge.

After spending four years as Forest Supervisor of the Lassen, I was transferred to the Regional office in San Francisco to the position of Assistant Chief, Division of Timber Management, in which capacity I am still serving.

Clarence E. Dunston

1615 Rhode Island Ave., N.W.,
Washington, D.C.
February 27, 1940.

Mr. C.E. Dunston,
U.S. Forest Service,
760 Market Street,
San Francisco, California.

Dear Mr. Dunston:

Because of Mr. Pinchot's unavoid-
able absence from Washington, he is unable
to handle his mail. He has asked me,
therefore, to write you how greatly he
appreciates your cooperation and to tell
you that you will hear from him personally
when he gets back. He asks you please to
forgive the delay.

Sincerely yours,

Secretary to Mr. Pinchot.

GP: AMB

1615 Rhode Island Ave., N.W.,
Washington, D.C.,
March 21, 1940.

Mr. C. E. Dunston,
760 Market St.,
San Fransisco, California.

Dear Mr. Dunston:

My best thanks for yours
of February 23, which would have been
acknowledged long ago had I not been off
on a cruise in the Caribbean. I appreciate it immensely, and I am very much in
your debt. I am delighted to be reminded
of the Heywood Trial. I had entirely forgotten the incident you described.

Your account of the drive on Clear-
water Creek is fascinating, and I am particularly glad to get in touch with Major Fenn
again through your story. I had the greatest
regard for him.

Well I remember the talk in the
upper room of the Forest Service the day after
I was fired, and generally I am very much in
your debt for your highly interesting account.

Faithfully yours,

GP

GP: AMB

chapter 5

Nils B. Eckbo

CALIFORNIA, UTAH, IDAHO, ARIZONA

1907-1919

"The beasts in question win not the noble lions, but the infernal bedbugs."

—Nils B. Eckbo

ils B. Eckbo sent a brief account of his work from Pretoria, South Africa that reached Gifford Pinchot at home in Milford as World War II raged across Europe. The Forest Service played an important role in the war effort, not just on the home front but wherever the Old Timers turned up. At the onset of war, however, conservation of the environment is generally placed on the back burner.

Nils B. Eckbo was born in Kristiana, Norway on February 4, 1885. The Yale Forest School directory notes that he descended from Vikings. He graduated from the Stenkjar Forest Academy in Norway in 1904, then worked as a lumberman in Maine and New Hampshire. In 1907, after studies at the Yale

Forest School, he joined the U.S. Forest Service in California, served in the Pacific Northwest, then went on to study forestry in Japan, Germany, Austria and Switzerland from July, 1908 until July 1909. Returning to the United States, Eckbo served in District 4 in Idaho, Utah and Arizona. He also served as a forest examiner on the Uinta National Forest with headquarters in Provo, Utah.

1229 Church Street,
Pretoria, South Africa.
21-5-40.

Dear Mr. Pinchot:

Your very kind letter dated Dec. 11 arrived some
time ago and I was both Delighted and flattered to be
asked to contribute to your book.

As much as I love to think back on my twelve years
service in the early days of the Forest Service, I
should equally love to commit some of the experiences
to a written record, but inspite of all this it has been
impossible for me to find the necessary time. Since
the outbreak of the war, the Forest Products Institute
here of which I am chief, has been inundated with extra duties until there is hardly time left to sleep.

An S.O.S. came through from Defense Headquarters
the other day saying that the troops at a certain camp
were being chewed up by nocturnal creatures, could we
help. The beasts in question win not the noble lions,
but the infernal bedbugs. Not long afterwards they
were toasting in our Seasoning Kilns at { } tempera-
tures, since then the troops have sung our praises.

In { } of the foregoing, you may pardon my inabil-
ity to fall in with your request so far, and will if
I should be able to find time in the not too distant
future it would no doubt be too late.

Most sincerely yours,

Nils B. Eckbo

July 9, 1940

Mr. Nils B. Eckbo,
1290 Church Street,
Pretoria, South Africa.

Dear Mr. Eckbo:

Many thanks for yours of May 21, which I have read with keenest interest.

Of course you have no time now to spend on anything but the war. In that you have my warmest sympathy and heartfelt wishes. I feel so strongly that about it that, if I could have my way, the United States would send everything it possibly could in the way of war materials to England and not charge a cent for them. The Brit Empire is fighting the fight of civilization and decency everywhere, and it is almost as necessary for us that you should win as it is for you.

Your story of the nocturnal enemy is most interesting. I hope you get rid of the diurnal one just as effectively.

With every good wish and high appreciation.

Sincerely yours,

GP

GP: AMB

chapter 6

Earle H. Frothingham

NEBRASKA, NORTH CAROLINA, COLORADO, UTAH, CONNECTICUT, WASHINGTON, D.C.

1906-1940

"I owe my first inclination toward forestry to an early passion for the study of birds."

—Earle H. Frothingham

*E*arle Hazeltine Frothingham was 60 years old in the summer of 1940 when he wrote Old Chief Pinchot from Biltmore Forest, North Carolina. He had retired not far from the site of the first American school of forestry, the Biltmore Forest School, established by George Vanderbilt in 1898 under the direction of German-born forester Carl Schenck.

"I am mortified at the scantiness of what I can offer," Frothingham wrote. "I have a rotten memory, and my diaries, which are pretty complete from 1906, are nothing but dry accounts of the minor incidents of field trips. The jobs to which I was assigned were technical ones, and I was preoccupied with them to the neglect of broader considerations. This does not mean that I was not constantly inspired by the struggles and successes of the Service under your leadership."

Earle H. Frothingham was born in Iowa in 1880 and graduated with an M.A. from the University of Michigan in July, 1906. Frothingham joined the Society of American Foresters in 1908 and served as its Secretary from 1910-1913, Treasurer in1921, and member of the Executive Council from 1923-1927.

Before taking charge of the Appalachian Forest Experiment Station in Asheville, North Carolina on July 1, 1921, he had served in the United States Forest Service for 15 years. The Appalachian Station, one of two forest experiment stations at the time, started out with "headquarters" at the Pisgah National Forest in one room with one staff member: Frothingham. He was later joined by four others including Josephine Laxton of Asheville, stenographer-typist; E.F. McCarthy, 36, a professor at the New York State College of Forestry appointed while serving as a research specialist in Canada; Ferdinand W. Haasis, who later became a botanist with the California Department of Forestry; and Clarence F. Korstian, a native of Nebraska who later became a Professor of Forestry at Duke University and the head of Duke Forest.

In his letter to Pinchot, Frothingham described a "pleasant recollection" in which meetings of the Baked Apple Club were held at 1615 Rhode Island Avenue, Washington, D.C., Gifford Pinchot's home. At one meeting in particular, Frothingham recalled a discussion in which "the problem of whether or not forests influence rainfall was solved by majority vote, and the subsequent meeting at which that action was rescinded."

As in a tennis match, Pinchot served the question over the net and the Old Timer sent the ball back with grace and appreciation. In each letter, we note a sense of civility, purpose, and caution taken not to offend. Each forester was a member of a family that cared for one another and valued the years spent together through struggle or triumph.

Frothingham's letter to his Old Chief stood out for its brevity. It also stood out for a single sentence standing sentinel at the door to the third paragraph:

"I owe my first inclination towards forestry to an early passion for the study of birds."

Birds. Imagine. Earl Hazeltine Frothingham was a young man in search of a mission. Fortunately, he found it early in the woods near his home. I pictured him hiking through a forest of bur oak with a chorus of birds singing from the branches overhead.

The Old Timers correspondence resonates like birdsong. The narratives are a call to our humanity and our willingness to serve the future aspirations of young people. They remind us of the fragility of life and that one place to heal our brokenness is through the restoration of landscapes, the protection of water, and the planting of trees.

#1 Lone Pine Road,
Biltmore Forest,
Biltmore, N. C.
July 10, 1940

Hon. Gifford Pinchot,
Milford, Pike Co., Pa.

Dear Mr. Pinchot:

I am awfully sorry to be nearly a month late in responding to your invitation of June 14 to relate my experiences in the Forest Service. Shortly after receipt of your letter I dug up my diaries for an early reply, but for the past two weeks I have had to be general factotum at home, with a house painting job under way and my wife sick in bed. She is improving, and I am able to resume the account of my not very impressive career in the Forest service.

I am mortified at the scantiness of what I can offer. I have a rotten memory, and my diaries, which are pretty complete from 1906, are nothing but dry accounts of the minor incidents of field trips. The jobs to which I was assigned were technical ones, and I was preoccupied with them to the neglect of broader considerations. This doesnt mean that I was not constantly inspired by the struggles and successes of the Service under your leadership. I vividly remember the thrill of being a member of an organization fighting against odds for such a cause. I made an attempt to express this in a paper I wrote for a local essay club a few years ago; Herbert Smith has read it, and can tell you that it doesn't contain anything that would be specific enough to be useful to you. I make this explanation so you won't have to waste your time on what follows.

I owe my first inclination toward forestry to an
early passion for the study of birds. When I began a course in
medicine at the University of Michigan, in 1900, I was not satisfied that I was on the right track. The outdoors was in
my blood. There was a rumor that a course in forestry was to
start at the University, and I had a yen to find out what it
would be like. I consulted your Primer of Forestry and Schlick's
Manual. They opened up a fascinating vista, and the die was cast.

I received my M.A. in forestry at the University
of Michigan in 1906, under the tutelage of "Daddy" Roth.
On July 1, 1906, I entered the Service at Halsey, Nebraska,
where I spent the summer and fall on the Old Dismal River
National Forest under the direction of Chas. A. Scott and
William Mast, in the Office of Forest Extension, which was
headed by E.A. Sterling. I decidedly did not distinguish
myself there. As you will remember, we were up against a
tough problem, trying to establish forest plantations under
conditions that we knew were bad, but didn't understand. One
of my associates there was Carlos Bates, to whose talent the
later success of the plantations was largely due. Success
came about chiefly through ceasing to pamper the planting
stock in the nursery and through adapting the stock to the
conditions of the planting sites.

In the fall of the 1906 I was summoned to Washington
where I was stationed until I came to Asheville, in 1921.
After a week or so in William L. Hall's Office of Forest
Products, studying lumber price trends, I was transferred
to the division of silvics, then in the Office of Publication
and Education, directed by Herbert A. Smith. Early in 1907
this division became the Office of Silvics, under Raphael Zon,
in the Branch of Silviculture, headed by William T. Cox.
My first job there was to write some of a series of "silvical
notes." These were brief summaries of as much of the pertin-

ent information about the characteristics and requirements
of the more important tree species as could be learned from the
meager literature then available. At your direction Findley
Burns described this and related work as follows: "The Service
sought scientists and secured several to seek sedulously the
silvical secrets secluded in several species, viewing vivacious-
ly the various varieties of virgin vegetation—." I wish
I could recall more of the delightful contacts I had at that
time with Herbert Smith, Zon, Burns, Treadwell Cleveland, and
others. They were more than kind to the unsophisticated infant
left on their doorstep. I was put in dubious charge
of a section of compilation for a couple of years.

From 1907 to 1914 I was in charge of a number of
field studies, leading to publications on a number of tree
species — Douglas Fir, in Colorado and Utah (1907); aspen,
assisting W.G. Weigle (1909); second-growth hardwoods in
Connecticut (1910); northern hardwoods and hemlock (1911-1914);
and white pine (1914). In 1914 I wrote a bulletin on farm
woodlots in Michigan, in cooperation with the State, and a
Forest Service bulletin on the "status and value of farm woodlots in the Eastern United States." The Douglas fir circular
was reprinted, in German, in the Deutsche Dendrologischen
Gesellschaft proceedings (1909). All these publications look
amateurish today, in the light of the advances that have
been made since then; and Zon used to say that all of them put
together were not as good as the poem I wrote entitled "Ask Zon."

From 1915 to 1917 I made studies in the Southern
Appalachians, of cut-over areas, forest conditions in relation
to the damage from the freshet of 1916, thinnings in the
Biltmore Estate plantations, and height growth of trees as an
index of site quality. Results of the cut-over study
were used as a guide to cutting practice on the national
forests of this region for a period. The Biltmore thinning

plots have been thinned four times, and I expect to write
them up next year, when the experiments will be 25 years old.
The study of height growth as a key to site (extension of an
idea of "Daddy" Roth's) led to the site index standards now
in general use.

From January through March, 1918, I was loaned
to the War Department for a fuel wood campaign in Michigan,
cooperating with A. K. Chittenden; and from May to December
of the same year I continued the war work by inspecting the
output of saw-mills, labor conditions, etc., relative to the
production of war materials, in Wisconsin and Michigan.

In 1920 I assisted in the preparation of the "Capper
Report," writing the sections on the Lake States and Southern
Appalachians, and in 1921 came down to Asheville to establish
the Appalachian Forest Experiment Station. I have lived in
Asheville ever since.

I joined the Society of American Foresters in 1908,
was Secretary from 1910 to 1913, Treasurer in 1921, and
member of the Executive Council from 1923 to 1927. As member
in charge of admissions I had the disagreeable task of invest-
igating the charges brought by H.H. Chapman against H.P. Baker,
finding in favor of the latter. A pleasanter recollection is
that of the "Baked Apple Club" meetings held at your home,
particularly the one at which the problem of whether or not
forests influence rainfall was solved by majority vote, and
the subsequent meeting at which that action was rescinded.

Such is the dull history of my service. I know it
will not be of any use to you, but it has been interesting to
me to write it out for the first time and my thanks are due
to you for the incentive. The old Service was a constant

inspiration. It still is. I remember Mr. Sherman's favorite quotation: "We who followed the Colonel, follow the Colonel still."

I shall be intensely interested in your annals, and I wish you the best of luck in finishing them. I had wonderful good fortune in being in the Service when you were at its head.

Very sincerely yours,

Earl H. Frothingham

P.S. I don't think I have any documents that would be worth preserving. I have (or had) letters from Heinrich Mayr and Dr. Schwappach about Douglas fir that I would be glad to send along if wanted, and if I can find them.

Office of Forest Extension.
From the narrative of Earle H. Frothingham. Library of Congress.
Manuscript Division. Gifford Pinchot Collection. Old Timers Collection.

July 13, 1940.

Mr. Earl H. Frothingham,
1 Lone Pine Road,
Biltmore Forest,
Biltmore, North Carolina.

Dear Frothingham:

Best thanks for yours of July 10.
Your story comes in plenty of time, and,
moreover, it's by no means a dull history.
If some of these days you fnd some anecdotes to add, I'll be glad to have them,
and I know they will very greatly add to
the record. In the meantime, what you say
about the Service in the old days is sure
true.

I was particularly delighted to get
that picture. I have been looking back
through the years to get to recognize these
faces through the mask of the way they look
now.

Any old records including those letters
from Mayr and Schwappach will be mighty welcome.

With hearty thanks,

Yours as always,

GP

GP:AMB

chapter 7

William L. Hall

Washington, D.C., North Dakota, South Dakota, Nebraska, Kansas, Oklahoma, Texas, Hawaii, California, Wisconsin
1899-1919

"As to the the personnel of the Forest Service, I have felt that I had the privilege of working with as fine a group of men as anywhere to be found."

—William L. Hall

For every young man who received a formal education at Yale Forest School, (endowed by James and Mary Pinchot in 1900), or who attended the Yale Forest School Camp in the woods behind the Pinchot summer home, Grey Towers, there was another who entered government service by taking the Civil Service exam and the outdoor test. Many young men and women came from circumstances of less privilege having grown up on a farm, ranch, or working in a sawmill. The criteria for entry was exacting and required, among other qualifications, physical endurance in the out of doors.

Physical hardship and outdoor challenges were once part of every American childhood. Life was a series of surprise encounters on Main Street or on the road from here to there. A flat tire. A fire to put out. A row to hoe led to a conversation that led to another conversation that led, potentially, to an adventure, a new discovery, or a job. Today, for so many reasons—from financial encumbrances to technological distractions—we have lost the "luxury" of wandering and encountering the unexpected event that might change our lives for the better.

Not knowing where success comes from, how it is earned, who planted a tree, where it grew, how it found its way to a sawmill or landfill, or how or whether it decayed and re-entered the duff on the forest floor, deprives us of connection to the substance of life itself. We know that education and skills are keys to a better life. But how do we navigate from here to there? From nothing to something? How many trees can one man plant in a day?

Nature was an inspiration for me from an early age. At four years old, my mother discovered a beautiful but isolated old mill for sale in the real estate section of the *New York Times*. At six years old, I found my way into the forest, making friends with trees, birds, and a fast-moving stream that emptied into what we called the "moat," a stone trough that once held the mill's waterwheel.

Like most children, I had no idea what was going on. My father came and went while my mother did her best to hold down the fort. My grandmother made me smocks of cotton, dying the fabric herself and sewing them by hand.

Like so many, my mother's mother, not my mother, made sure I got to school on time. She took us on picnics, taught me how to cook and sew, and led me around her garden filled with for-get-me-nots, lily of the valley, roses, and raspberries. She was terribly and terrifically practical. In shop class I learned wood-working, making napkin holders, cutting boards, and small wooden tables. I was happy to come home from school with something to do, always gluing and clamping broken furniture together or painting things. I wanted things to look presentable on the outside even if they were messy on the inside.

In 1972, after my parents divorce, we moved to a house not far from the mill and the moat. I loved the outdoors and color so I planted a ring of zinnias and marigolds that reminded me of the sunflowers we'd had at the mill. We were poor in a sea of rich, a badge of shame in an American childhood.

I left home early, honing my survival skills. At 17, I enrolled at college in New Orleans where I learned to buckle down and study but also how to dance and enjoy life. I needed a career and a way to support myself, so in 1983 I entered graduate school in landscape architecture with loans and grants and a part-time job in the library. Upon graduation in 1986, we were a small, migratory flock of landscape architects moving wherever we could find work. I drove west pitching my tent by the side of the road, pulling out a map and compass, navigating the high-ways and byways of America by myself.

In the summer of 1990, I wandered into the Portland, Oregon office of the U.S. Forest Service. I wasn't quite sure of my connection to Gifford Pinchot at the time. At the top of my list of life's mysteries was the missing family tree. During my visit with the landscape architect in charge of Region 6, I was told of a job opening on the Mt. Hood National Forest.

Forest Guards planting trees on old Oregon National Forest. 1914

From the narrative of Albert Wiesendanger. Library of Congress.
Manuscript Division. Gifford Pinchot Collection. Old Timers Collection.

WILLIAM L. HALL

CONSULTING FORESTER

900 PROSPECT AVENUE

HOT SPRINGS ARKANSAS

Great Southern Hotel
Meridian, Mississippi
June 27, 1940

Mr. Gifford Pinchot,
Milford, Pennsylvania.

Dear Mr. Pinchot:

Some weeks ago when your letter came out in
the *Journal of Forestry* requesting assistance of pioneer
foresters in building up the record of the early work in
forestry in the United States, I realized that I had an
obligation in that direction that should not be shirked.
Then, when your personal letter, dated June 14th, came
it not only strengthened my feeling of obligation, but
aroused a desire to give what practical help I can. Being
away from home your letter was delayed in reaching me and
I have thought the matter over a few days before replying.
I do want to help and will undertake to do so. Away from
home and hindered somewhat by not having at hand certain
early records, which might be of help, I will endeavor to
make a start on my part this coming weekend.

My fear is that my narrative may string out
into quite a lengthy story. There is much that could be
said of this period of boyhood and early manhood before I
entered the Division of Forestry, and there is much that
could be said of my work in the old Bureau of Forestry
between 1899 and 1905, because I personally carried

almost sole responsibility for several projects that later became important.

It has been in my mind in recent years to piece together the story of my own participation in forestry. The record now covers more than forty years, the first half of which was in public service, the second half in private work. Never during the entire period have I been out of work. Always there have been a lot of things waiting to be done. My contacts, of course, have been wide, and I have met many points of view.

Feeling that you have undertaken a work of great importance, I shall be glad to help. During the more than forty years of our friendship I have ever had for you the highest regard, and I can truthfully say you stimulated me in early life more than any other person.

Consequently my highest regards and best wishes,

Yours sincerely,

Wm. L. Hall

WH:lc

July 1, 1940.

Mr. William L. Hall,
Great Southern Hotel,
Meridian, Mississippi.

Dear Hall:

Best thanks for yours of
June 27. Let your narrative go just
as long as it will, the longer the
better. That is just what I want.
And take your time.

Every good wish,

Yours as always,

GP

GP:AMB

WILLIAM L. HALL

CONSULTING FORESTER

900 PROSPECT AVENUE

HOT SPRINGS ARKANSAS

September 3, 1940.

Mr. Gifford Pinchot,
Milford, Pennsylvania.

Dear Mr. Pinchot:

Nearly complete is my narrative of my early experiences which led me into forestry and my work in the Forest Service during the twenty years I was a member of that organization. The account runs to about 55 typed pages.

On a few dates that I want to bring in I am in doubt, and I have written to several men who can, I am sure, help me to supply them. As soon as their replies are received, I can forward the manuscript to you.

I have no thought that you will want to use this narrative, or any considerable part of it, as part of the book which you have in preparation. My only thought is that my account may have in it information which may be helpful to you in preparation of your book. This word is sent merely that you may know that I have been at work on the matter, and that my narrative will soon be in your hands.

With best regards,

Sincerely yours,

Wm. L. Hall

WLH:lc

September 6, 1940.

Mr. William L.Hall,
900 Prospect Avenue,
Hot Springs, Arkansas.

Dear Hall:

Hearty thanks for yours of
September 3. I am delighted you are going to send me your story. Whether or
not I can use it or any part of it (as I
expect to do) in my book, its principal
value is going to be in supplying material
for the ultimate story of forestry in the
United States and your part in it. For
that reason I am very greatly pleased that
you are working it out and are going to
let me have it. Many thanks to you.

Yours as always,

GP

GP:AMB

WILLIAM L. HALL
CONSULTING FORESTER
900 PROSPECT AVENUE
HOT SPRINGS ARKANSAS

The Great Southern Hotel,
Meridian, Mississippi,
September 21, 1940

Mr. Gifford Pinchot,
Milford, Pike County,
Pennsylvania.

Dear Mr. Pinchot:

Herewith is the statement I have worked out concerning mainly my connection with the Federal forestry work between 1899 and 1919. While it was your request that started me on this statement, I have had two objectives in view in its preparation. With one of these you are not at all concerned.

My hope is that the statement will be of help to you in presenting some of the salient facts connected with these parts of the forestry work in which I was engaged in the twenty year period. Please feel free to make any use of the information that you may wish. It has been a pleasure to give this small assistance in the splendid work you are doing. If I can be of further assistance, please let me know.

With best personal regards,

Sincerely yours,

Wm. L. Hall

WLH : lc

WHAT I HAVE SEEN, FELT AND TRIED TO DO IN FORESTRY
By William L. Hall

AS A BOY

My earliest recollections cluster around fields and
trees. My Father was a farmer in west central Missouri.
In addition to his 160 acres of fresh fertile farm land
he had acquired some two or three hundred acres of more
rugged land, largely covered by timber. My first memories
are of those fields and woods. Well I recall my seventh
birthday. My father sent me out to a back field in the
afternoon with the hired man to hoe corn. Hoeing corn is
no picnic for any boy of seven years, and that being a warm
late May afternoon I soon felt that a little relaxation
was desirable, so the hired man and I betook ourselves
to a nearby shady Osage Orange hedge row. He sprawled
on the ground, shading his eyes with his hat, while I
busied myself trying to dig out a crayfish. Suddenly,
came a voice, "Willie, what are you doing here?" It was
my Mother on horseback on a way to a neighboring farm.
This challenge broke up a very pleasant interlude in the
afternoon. That evening, I well remember, that my Mother
had for me a birthday cake, but my father had for me a
spanking. Another day a little later my Father, having
just acquired an additional piece of land, took me with
him to look it over. I recall that it had around the edges

some rather unsightly brushy woods, but toward the center was an attractive little field. When we had looked it over I summed up my impressions by remarking, "This place is like a nut, best inside." My Father thought this quite a bright remark, and reminded me of it at various times later. For that reason, I suppose, it has stuck in my memory.

One of my most vivid recollections of that early period was of a little sawmill that my Father owned, or hired, I do not remember which. He ran it between crop seasons, going about three miles from home for this timber work. During the winter months, when the days were short, he would leave home before day, and of course, get back after dark. I well remember a good many days spent with him. Some of the winter mornings were cold with an abundance of snow on the ground. But once at the mill we built a fire and the hours went pleasantly by. That was the time of the appearance of Haley's comet in the early eighties. I remember well that unusual spectacle of the early morning skies, the great tail streaming far across the heavens. Other recollections of this episode are of huge white oak trees that were cut into logs, brought to the mill and made into lumber. It seemed a very wonderful process to see a tree cut into material that could be used in building a house. It was a vivid lesson in the adaption of natural materials to man's needs. Also, well remembered was a little deposit of coal that outcropped along a creek

in my Father's timberlands. This coal bed was only 8" to
10" thick. My Father thought that by a little excavation
work he might find the vein to increase in thickness.
Nothing came of it, but this exploration work to me was
very fascinating.

Again I remember my Father's fields for I was
constantly over them in connection with the farm work.
I was water-boy and had to keep the field force supplied
with cool drinking water. The surface of the farm lands
was gently rolling, and I can remember after heavy rains
the little riverlets of water cutting into the soil; thus
came my first observation of soil erosion.

These things I vividly remember and mention them
here to show that my earliest impressions were of things
outside—the fields, soil, woods, minerals. Of people and
other things such as school and play and early associates,
I have no such vivid recollections. This early period
of my life closed with two years residence in a small
town. Neither did the town life make much impression on
my mind. I, of course, went to school, had playmates and
participated in summer and winter sports common to boys
of ten to twelve years of age. It may be interjected here
that boys of that period had a greater variety of simple
games than do boys of today. We had no movies then.

When I was nearing thirteen years of age, my Father
moved his family to the plains of southern Kansas. Here
were new contacts with nature. Well remembered is the

turning up of the fresh prairie soil which no plow had penetrated before. Being an only son, from this time on it was up to me to take full share of the heavy work of the farm and much of this prairie land I broke up myself. That portion of Kansas was naturally treeless except for thin ribbons of cottonwoods and willow, along the small sandy streams. The exploring of these streams in our immediate locality provided much adventure. This was the active period of the Federal timber culture program. Our neighborhood was new, the first settlers had possessed their lands only ten or twelve years before, and some of these lands were taken up under the Timber Culture Act. Plantations of trees were springing up, mostly cottonwood. To me it was a striking revelation that men could actually go out and by his own activity bring a forest into existence. I had not before realized it could be done.

This period of my life covered two years—from the age of thirteen to fifteen. A most vivid recollection is of a successful Arbor Day celebration in the town school which I attended. Under the inspiration of an unusually active superintendent we made quite a day of it. Rubbish had to be raked up and hauled away, flower beds had to be spaded up and made ready for planting, and shrubs and trees were to be set out. Where the planting material came from is not remembered but I do recall, that when the day was over, our school ground was much improved in appearance. The

start made that day was never completely lost. It was my
proud privilege to furnish my father's team and wagon
to haul away rubbish, and do the other hauling required
in the day's activity. Naturally after that experience it
might be supposed that I would have a warm place in my
heart for Arbor Day. I may add, that years later while in
the Division of Forestry, I had the pleasure of visiting
Honorable J. Sterling Norton, founder of Arbor Day, at
his home on the bluffs of the Missouri River in eastern
Nebraska. To Mr. Morton I recounted this experience of
mine, and he took me over his interesting timber belts
and explained how he had extended them by protecting the
squirrels, which became his tree planters.

The wanderlust came again to my Father. In Colorado
were free lands—limitless acres. They called him and
my father trekked west again with all his belongings.
Not much of this world's goods, but household stuff and
essential tools and implements to fill several wagons, and
these followed by a pretty herd of some 40 black polled
Angus cattle. Well remembered were those travels—300
miles over rolling plains, across sand-bedded streams
with merely newly-made trails for roads. Established in
our new home, came more than a year in a half dugout, half
adobe, sod-covered home, with only chalky clay sub soil
for a floor. Not a companion of my own age, only a horse
and a dog; not a tree in sight of that home. But 10 miles
to the westward were the blue foothills of the Rockies,

pinon and juniper covered. To these foothills we went for wood, and there for me was endless romance. Often I was there alone, and many things I saw. Once I ran across the skeleton of a cow that had wedged a foot in the crevice of a rock, had never been able to get loose, and the poor thing died there. The tragedies of nature came to me afresh with that observation. On the other hand, how lovely were those foothills with their pinons and junipers!

Here in Southeastern Colorado, in what became the Dust Bowl, came my first practical experience in forestry. I was just turning sixteen, and in addition to a homestead and a section of school land, my Father had taken up a timber claim which we planned to win by establishing a tree plantation upon it. Mine to turn up that prairie sod, go to the foothill arroyas and help gather cottonwood twigs for cuttings and stick them into the fresh virgin soil newly turned up. Not one of these, I suppose, lived out the first year, for this ill conceived adventure ended disastrously. Undependable water supply wrecked it.

This year on the Colorado plains left indelible impressions on me. I got used to being alone. Never since have I had a sense of loneliness when in the woods or fields or desert by myself. Never have I had any aptness in conversation. The small opportunity for conversation in that period may somewhat account for that. It was the time when I should have been in training.

While we were in our Colorado home came my first
contact with a Government field party. A Geological
Survey party came along and camped for a few weeks near
our place. They purchased from my mother butter, milk
and eggs, and welcomed or tolerated me on my visits to the
camp. Such commodious camp facilities I had never seen. I
was tremendously impressed. It would be a very wonderful
thing I thought to be a member of a Government field party
and live such a life. The party shortly moved and camped
next in the extreme northeastern part of New Mexico,
some 25 miles away. I remember riding early one Sunday
morning, saddling my horse, and riding the 25 miles down
and the 25 miles back to have a last short visit with that
party.

Back to Kansas went my Father, a sadder but wiser, much
wiser man. That experience cured his roaming fever for
good and all. Back again where there were schools, my own
thoughts turned seriously now to an education. I entered
school, beginning somewhere in the grammar grades. I
recall that after my long vacation school seemed very drab
and dull. Still living on a farm it was necessary to ride
four and one-half miles to school. Interest picked up a
little as I become better acquainted with my classmates
and got further into my studies. In the Geography we sued
there was a picture of the Administration Building of the
Kansas State Agricultural College. How lovely it would
be, I thought, to go to school and study in a building like

that with hundreds of other students. But that building
was far away, 200 miles or more. One had to go on the train
and to ride the train cost money, a lot more money than I
had in sight. Another boy I knew did go, and after a time
came home and told us wonderful stories of college life
and surroundings, and the way the students worked, how
they prepared themselves for lives of usefulness, and
after graduation went to varied fields of work in widely
scattered places. This was the first personal account I had
ever had of college life, and I had never seen a college. It
powerfully stimulated my imagination.

AS A STUDENT

In two or three years more, at the age of 19, I finished
High School. Strong in my mind was the determination
to go to the Kansas State Agricultural College; no other
institution was thought of. And it was beyond hope to
spend more than a term or two at college. The previous fall
my Father had made available to me a rented field of about
twelve acres for a crop of wheat. I worked diligently on it,
got it seeded in good time and in good condition, and the
following summer, soon after I finished High School, I was
rewarded with an average harvest, which netted me $90.
Thus was financed my start in college.

Then came experiences never to be forgotten, those
first days in autumn of 1892 in the halls of a real college.

To be in a surging crowd of students--500 or more--what
a joyous, driving experience. I felt a bursting sense of
growth as a young tree possibly feels in springtime. But
this young student was weak--painfully weak--on the
financial side. Everything had to be done to guard the
little hoard with which he started. Living was cheap in
those days at that Kansas College. After considerable
looking around I found that the lowest cost meals I could
get were $1.50 per week. It took ingenuity to work out
an almost costless room arrangement. Finding another
student in about the same financial status as myself we
looked around together. Finally we found a flimsy little
two-room cottage, with one room vacant and unfurnished.
This we rented at $2.00 a month.

Then came a hunt for work. No work appeared until late
in the fall when I was given a few days employment in the
Agricultural Department.

Meanwhile, bad news came from home. My Mother was
in rapidly failing health. As weeks went by worse and
worse came the news from home and lower and lower and
lower went my funds. By the end of the winter term there
was no longer a question as to what I should do, I must go
home. Dark days followed. But it has ever been a solace to
remember that I was at my Mother's side during the last few
weeks of her life.

My Father and I were left alone. A man and a boy alone
on the farm have a tough time of it. We cooked our meals,

we washed our clothes, we kept our house, we worked the
farm. I don't remember that we complained very much about
it, but those were the drabbest days of my whole life. How
could I ever break out of it? We had a Seth Thomas clock
that set on a shelf and ticked very loudly in that little
farm house. Morning, noon and night I heard it ticking
away the hours, days, weeks, months. Free as anyone in the
world I was yet a prisoner.

In late summer came the first glimmer of hope. The
local district school would need a new teacher. Far from
my mind was the desire to teach school, but something
had to be done. I sent to the County Teacher's Institute
for four weeks, took an examination and passed. To the
local director of the school I went. Two were somewhat
sympathetic, but quite non-committal. The third was a
tough old character, uneducated, and addicted to the most
terrific profanity. Listening to my story he was quite
silent for a few months, sent a heavy stream of tobacco
juice far down the road and answered, "Billy, if you want
that school I'm (here as fancy a flow of outlaw English as I
ever heard, but what followed was like heavenly music to
me) "you can count on me to leg for you."

The school was mine, eight months of it, at $40.00 a
month. Living at home with my Father and doing everything
for ourselves, I finished the term about $200.00 to the
good and in the fall of 1894 back to college I went—a

young man with confidence vastly revived. I was indeed
walking on air.

Not many weeks passed before I had some work in the
Horticultural Department, in the college. That was just
what I wanted. I wanted to work with trees. Everything
that came to me to do was interesting. Before long I was
working every afternoon and Saturdays. Doing all my
studying at night and in the early morning, I got on very
well. Having no time to spend money except for the most
necessary things I soon was managing to keep my grades
well up. I never have required more than six and one-
half hours sleep and that helped greatly in these days of
arduous work and study.

Beginning in 1895, summer vacation periods were also
spent at work in the college orchards and gardens. I was a
student with regular spare-time department employment.
In studies I specialized more and more in horticultural
and related subjects and in the sciences. Head of the
Horticultural Department was Silas C. Mason who became a
most helpful friend and advisor. Professor Mason himself
inclined strongly towards forestry. By the time I was a
junior he was conducting classes in forestry, depending
altogether upon foreign textbooks, but having nearby
timber belts and forest plantations for field study. These
courses I struck at as eagerly as a hungry trout takes a
fly.

FIRST WORK IN FORESTRY

In 1895, the Federal Division of Forestry had
developed plans for an extensive series of experimental
forest plantings in cooperation with a number of State
Experimental Stations of the middle west, the Kansas
Station being one. Purpose of these experiments was to
test out various species mixtures in plantations. While
Dr. B. E. Fernow was then Chief of the Division of Forestry,
Mr. Charles A. Kefer was Assistant Chief and organized and
directed these treeplanting experiments. The Federal
Government furnished plans and planting stock, the local
stations did the planting, took charge of the plantations
when established and kept records, making periodic
reports on results.

From the first I was in on this work and took to it
with great relish. About that time I was made a student
assistant and took charge of a squad of workers, mostly
students. I saw much of Mr. Keffer on his frequent visits
to the Kansas station, and I recall one or two visits by Dr.
Fernow. They were the first foresters I ever met.

All through my student days I was conscious that I was
only a farm boy in an agricultural college. I assumed that
in the leading universities much better training was to
be had and much better students were to be found. Whether
this was an illusion or whether it was true never has been
entirely clear to me.

The year 1898 was a memorable one in forestry in the
United States. In that year Dr. Fernow relinquished his
position as Chief of the Forestry Division and became
head of the School of Forestry at Cornell. Gifford Pinchot
became Chief of the Division of Forestry. In fact, the
directive personnel of the Division of Forestry almost
completely changed during the summer of 1898. A few
months later, Professor James Toumey, of the University
of Arizona, was called to Washington to take charge of
the western activities of the Division. One of Toumey's
first duties was to inspect the plantations established
in cooperation with the Western Experiment stations and
determine whether or not they should be continued. In
course of time Professor Toumey on his inspection came
to the Kansas Station. It was my privilege to go over the
plantations with him, show him the results and discuss the
future of the project. My recollection is that Professor
Toumey's visit to Kansas was in June 1899. It was a few days
after my college had closed.

After the inspection was completed and we had fully
discussed the treeplanting project, he outlined to me
another project that he and Mr. Pinchot were considering
with a view to its replacing the planting project carried
on in cooperation with several Experiment Stations. This
was a plan to extend direct cooperation of the Federal
Government to individual landowners in establishing
plantations. The underlying thought was that with the

interest in tree planting, especially in the west, under
the stimulus of the Timber Claim Act, landowners might
be quite ready to establish plantations for themselves if
they could be aided by advice and plans from the Federal
Government. On a warm afternoon we sat for two hours, I
suppose, in the shade of a big apple tree on the college
campus and thrashed out this subject. Professor Toumey
finally told me that this project would, no doubt, be put
underway. He said that the Civil Service examination
for Superintendent of Treeplanting had already been
scheduled to be held within a few weeks. He suggested
that I take that examination. I do not remember that I
committed myself in the matter in that talk, but as I
look back now over a stretch of 41 years I realize that
my decision to go into forestry was made on that June
afternoon as I talked with Professor Toumey on the campus
of the Kansas State College.

AS A FEDERAL FORESTER

When the examination came in a few weeks later I took
it in Kansas City. It was in September before information
came that I had passed. In early September, about the time
I was to leave for Ithaca, notification was received that
I had passed the Civil Service Examination. Shortly I
received from Professor Toumey an offer of the position of
Assistant Superintendent of Treeplanting in the Division

of Forestry. I did not wholly give up the idea of going
to Cornell, but decided to go by way of Washington for
conferences with Professor Toumey and the Chief of the
Division of Forestry.

To the best of my recollection Professor Toumey was
absent when I arrived in Washington, but Gifford Pinchot
was there and I had an immediate talk with him. One hour
with that engaging personality was enough. I threw in my
lot with the Division of Forestry in what proved to be a
twenty year term. My employment in the Division began
September 16, 1899.

In his interview with me Mr. Pinchot confirmed the
word Professor Toumey had given me about the proposal
to encourage forest plantations throughout the country
by landowners, under stimulation and guidance of the
Federal Department. And he parallelled tht project with
another of farther- reaching significance, which was
the development of working plans for forest properties
for the guidance and stimulation of private timberland
owners.

These two lines of activity had already been
determined upon and announced. They were being organized
as far as men and funds were available. For the Fiscal
Year 1900 a considerable increase in appropriations for
the Division of Forestry had been made, thus beginning
a period of growth which has continued without much
interruption through four decades.

My work in the Division of Forestry was to be with
tree-planting activities. Professor Toumey was my Chief.
He returned to Washington within a day or two after my
arrival, and thereafter, we spent much time together,
carefully going over the situation so far as tree-
planting needs and opportunities were concerned, and
finally shaping plans for getting the project underway.
Announcement of the cooperative plans a few weeks earlier
had brought a number of responses. Nearly all were from
the middle west and mostly from the plains. Developing
plans indicated an early field trip for me.

Those few weeks in Washington were to me invaluable.
First they gave me the opportunity to become acquainted
with the men who were to be my fellow workers. Henry S.
Graves, Assistant Chief of the Division, and Overton W.
Price were two of these. Both of them, as was true with Mr.
Pinchot, had had the advantage of training in the best
forest schools of Germany and France. George B. Sudworth
was another man of wide scientific attainment with whom I
was to be closely associated during the next twenty years.
Chief Clerk of the Division was Otto Luebkert, a cultured
German, who had long been a resident of Washington. His
cordial friendship and ever-ready helpfulness aided me
greatly in getting established in surroundings entirely
new. Another man who became my warm friend within a short
time was the draftsman of the Division, E. H. Stuck, also
a German. I had much to learn on ways of getting along

in a governmental office and I do not believe I ever gave
sufficient thanks to these two men for their help extended
in so many ways.

These few weeks also helped me to get the feel of
eastern surroundings. I had never before been in the
East and everything was different from anything I had
been used to. In fact, I was only six year removed from
that little quiet Kansas house, from which it looked at
the time as though I might never escape. These six years
had done much for me. They had brought me the thrill of
accomplishment in the preparation for work, and they had
brought me to participation in an undertaking that would
most assuredly have national importance. Naturally I was
imbued with great zeal for the work before me.

PLANTING PLANS FOR PRIVATE OWNERS

About the middle of October, 1899, I started on my
first field trip. Being autumn I went first to North
Dakota and gradually worked southward through South
Dakota, Nebraska, Kansas, to Oklahoma and Texas. Advance
appointments had been made with the landowners I was to
visit, so they were expecting me. In all cases they turned
out to be substantial citizens with an earnest desire to
improve their home surroundings. Some of them wanted
wind-breaks; some wanted to grow trees suitable for fence
posts. There was a considerable variety of objectives. In

each case I found out what the man wanted to do. If I could help him in crystallizing his ideas as to some practical plan, I tried to do so. With the objectives clearly in mind we went about a study of the site with necessary measurements and sketches, and then discussed the extent of the planting to be undertaken, how the ground should be prepared and the work carried on.

Planting stock was a problem. At that time there were no public nurseries. All planting materials had to be obtained from private nurseries, and generally the cost of the required planting stock was considerable. A few of the plantings involved conifers, such as Red Cedar and Scotch Pine, but for the most part the plans called for deciduous trees such as American Elm, Green Ash, Hackberry, and in southern portion of the plains, Catalpa, Mulberry, Cottonwood and Boxelder. Plans were not completed in the field, but were worked out in the rough. This trip was finished and I returned to Washington at the end of the year. It took several weeks to complete the plans with necessary sketches and diagrams for planting trees. When completed they were forwarded to the landowner.

Meanwhile further publicity about the work brought many more applications and these later applications came not only from the middle West but from all parts of the United States except the South, where at that time there was no thought of tree planting. There were numerous applications from the North Central States and New

England. We, therefore planned for an active field season in 1900. Expansion of plans was made possible by a larger appropriation made available July 1 for the next fiscal year.

Late in 1899 came a new turn in forestry. While on my first field trip plans had been finally worked out in Washington for establishment of a School of Forestry at Yale University. The original gift which made this possible was from the family of Gifford Pinchot, Chief of the Division of Forestry. By the time of my return to Washington, around January 1, 1900, it was determined that Henry S. Graves and James W. Toumey would withdraw from the Division to organize and man the new school.

FIRST STUDIES OF FOREST PLANTATIONS

On that same date came organization of the first field party to study the history and growth of forest plantations. The work for that season was confined to the State of Kansas which provided a good number of plantations for studies. A three man party was organized, all of the men freshly graduated from western schools. None had studied forestry. The party was outfitted with a wagon and team with a driver who was also a cook for the little party. They had a tent and were prepared to settle down at any place the work required and stay for several days.

Beginning July 1, 1901 a party was organized to study forest plantations in the State of Nebraska. In this party were seven men, six of them later distinguished themselves in some branch of forestry. R.S. Kellogg was Chief of party, L.C. Miller Assistant Chief. Other members were Hugh P. Baker, John H. Hatton, E.P. Bailey, and F.G. Miller. The driver and cook for this party was Charles A. Scott, a graduate of the Kansas State College. Finishing his season with this field party, he obtained a position in the tree-planting work of the Bureau of Forestry and became a prominent figure in tree-planting operations during the first decade of this century Later he served the State of Kansas in its forestry activities. At present he is a nurseryman in Kansas.

The party was well equipped for its work. In adequacy of equipment it reminded me somewhat of the Geological Survey party which I saw in Colorado in my boyhood days. The party traveled widely in Nebraska, visited many plantations, making growth studies and also giving much consideration to planting opportunities in that State. Its most notable discovery was of a small plantiation of Jack Pine on a remote ranch near the Niobrara River in the sandhill section of Northern Nebraska. This plantation, though less than an acre in extent, showed beyond question the adaptability of Jack Pine to Nebraska sandhills.

Another important disclosure was that great areas
of the sandhills were still part of the public domain.
These two discoveries led to much consideration of the
possibilities of tree-planting in the sandhill region and
were responsible a few months later for the withdrawal of
two large areas from settlement. In 1902 these areas were
set aside as forest reserves. Tree-planting was started on
what was then considered a large scale at Halsey in 1903.
In 1927 the Forest Service held a silver anniversary for
this unique project. This Nebraska tree-planting project
resulted directly from work of the field party in 1901. In
turn the project greatly advance the conception of forest
planting on the forest reserves.

From the first Mr. Pinchot sought to inculcate a
spirit of comradeship and zeal of accomplishment in the
rapidly increasing force of the Division of Forestry. He
set a high standard of excellence of work, and sought by
every means to give his assistants vision of the great
program to be put underway. His powers of leadership
were extraordinary and his friendly and aggressive
personality was a powerful spur to all his workers. A man
of large means, and at the time, a bachelor, he used most
effectively his spacious home in Washington to advance
the interests of forestry. Early in 1900 he was gathering
members of his organization in weekly meetings at his
home to discuss problems of forestry, or lines of activity

which were underway. Usually addresses were given with lantern slides.

These meetings soon led to consideration of the advisability of an organization to include the professional foresters of the country. Interest in the proposal crystallized rapidly and at a meeting at the Pinchot home November 10, 1900, steps were taken to form an organization. The name, as chosen at subsequent meeting, was "The Society of American Foresters." Seven men organized the society and became its charter members, the writer being one of the group. The organization thus founded has had continuous existence, has grown through the years and has long been a powerful influence in the advancement of forestry in America. The question may be asked why so few men participated in the organization meeting. The explanation is that most members of the Division of Forestry were still in the field, not having returned to Washington from their season;s work. In these early meetings held at Mr. Pinchot's home, refreshments were always the same--baked apples, gingerbread and milk. Soon this gathering came to be known as 'The Baked Apple Club." These meetings were often attended by prominent scientists and public men. Theodore Roosevelt while President attended one or more meetings.

Twenty years in the Forest Service had brought to me a variety of advantages. They had given me the advantage of travel in every state in the Union; an opportunity

to work for considerable periods of time in many of the
states. I thus was able to acquire considerable knowledge
of our country, and especially I had opportunity to gain a
rather comprehensive understanding of forest conditions
in all parts of the United States. Another advantage which
through the years I have greatly appreciated was the
opportunity of making many close friends and many more
personal acquaintances throughout the United States. As
to the personnel of the Forest Service I have felt that I
had the privilege of working with as fine a group of men as
anywhere could be found. They were men of highest ideals,
many of unusual ability and outlook upon life. There was
great stimulation in this association, and I am glad to
give testimony to the benefits I derived from it.

September 27, 1940.

Mr. William L. Hall,
The Great Southern Hotel,
Meridian, Mississippi.

Dear Hall:

On my return I find your welcome
letter of September 21 and your most
interesting account of your work in forestry.
I am delighted with it and delighted to have
it, and I was particularly pleased with your
statement about the character of the men whom
you worked with in the Forest Service. That
agrees with my own experience absolutely.

Every good wish to you and renewed
thanks,

Yours as always,

GP

GP:AMB

chapter 8

R. Aldo Leopold

Arizona, New Mexico, Wisconsin

1909-1933

"It is unlikely that any one book, even from your pen, will capture all the angles of the story, and perhaps a generation or two must elapse before its values can be truly weighed by anyone."

—R. Aldo Leopold

The important thing," Aldo Leopold said, "is to strive." In his one-page letter to Pinchot and Pinchot's one paragraph response, we are left with more questions than answers. Did Rand Aldo Leopold, considered the father of wildlife conservation, and one of Pinchot's "Old Timers," complete his narrative? Author Wallace Stegner called Leopold a prophet. Had Leopold given up on Pinchot's definition of conservation by the time he received the Old Chief's letter or was he too busy to provide a longer contribution?

These and other questions resonate as we face the extinction of species, the contamination of water, and the destruction of forests worldwide. The philosophical underpinning of

Leopold's wilderness idea was no doubt formed in response to what, by 1920, was already apparent: wilderness designation was not enough to save us from ourselves.

Today, we might attempt the resurrection of species but we may not regain or recreate the habitat needed to sustain the mosaic of life on earth. The hunter who kills the wolf expresses no remorse. Leopold and Pinchot shared this insight into the nature of human beings. We share a common fate with those who plot the destruction of animals and rip up shallow topsoil in order to harvest the last wild lavender. The question is how soon and what will we do, individually and collectively, to prepare the next generation for the road ahead.

UNIVERSITY OF WISCONSIN

COLLEGE OF AGRICULTURE
MADISON, WISCONSIN

DEPARTMENT OF WILDLIFE MANAGEMENT

424 University Farm Place
January 4, 1940

Mr. Gifford Pinchot
Milford
Pike County
Pennsylvania

Dear Chief:

    I applaud your proposal to write a history of the Service, and especially your proposal to preserve historical materialsin the Library of Congress. It is unlikely that any one book, even from your pen, will capture all the angles of the story, and perhaps a generation or two must elapse before its values can be truly weighed by anyone.

    Unfortunately I have not kept a diary, and any attempt of mine to comply with your request as a whole would soon become a book rather than a letter. I am trying to single out what more limited contribution from me would be most useful to you.

    I take it you want to write a critical as well as a factual account of the Forest Service idea. If so, I am quite sure that my best contribution would be on the critical side. Do you want me to attempt a history of Forest Service thought, as exemplified in the Southwestern Region, up to World War I or thereabouts? Actually the year 1920 marks a turning point from (what shall I call it? a certain viewpoint, as yet unnamed) to an ecological mode of thinking. I am willing to attempt this, although I make no promises as to the value of the result. Of course I would illustrate this abstract treatment with local concrete events. Let me know whether this might fit in.

               Yours cordially,

             Aldo Leopold

             Aldo Leopold
       Professor of Wildlife Management

1615 Rhode Island Ave., N.W.,
Washington, D.C.,
January 10, 1940.

Dr. Aldo Leopold,
Professor of Wildlife Management,
424 University Farm Place,
University of Wisconsin,
Madison, Wisconsin.

Dear Leopold:

Best thanks for yours of
January 4. What I want is whatever
you would like to give me, history,
or criticism, or whatever you like.
I shall be immensely interested in a
critical account of the Forest Service
idea. Take your time, if I may suggest
it, and make your story full rather
than soon.

With all good wishes and
highest appreciation.

Sincerely yours,

GP

GP: AMB

chapter 9

Thornton T. Munger

PENNSYLVANIA, WASHINGTON D.C., OREGON, AND REGION 6 (PORTLAND) 1903–?

"The government expects to find some way to improve conditions by cutting the trees in a different manner. Of course it will take a long time to bring about the change, say 50 or 100 years, but Uncle Sam is in the forestry business for all time to come and he has become accustomed to looking a long way ahead."

—Thornton T. Munger

The Old Chief was eager to receive responses from the Old Timers. At 72, every day was precious and every page reminded him of what he had tried to do to help improve the lives of others. Each narrative was a gift from the past. It took courage for the Old Timers to summon their memories and recount what had happened so long ago.

One letter reminded Pinchot of the time he'd stood before a Colorado cattlemen's convention as the audience tried to boo him off stage. Eventually the crowd went silent, clinging to their seats and hanging on his every word. Others recalled the dramatic events surrounding his removal as Chief, and the terrible feeling of loss that ensued.

Old Timer Thornton Taft Munger was born October 3, 1883 in North Adams, Massachusetts, the son of a Congregational clergyman. He was one of the few Old Timers who was older than the Old Chief himself. In his narrative of 15 pages, Munger recalled that it was his sister, Eleanor, who suggested a career in forestry. Her idea made perfect sense. Their father owned a house in New Haven, Connecticut across from Hillhouse Woods, a park with a plant laboratory where young Thornton developed an early interest in the natural sciences and the collection of native plants and flowers.

Munger graduated from Yale University in 1905, went to Europe to continue his studies in forestry for nine months, then returned to the Yale School of Forestry where he completed a masters in forestry in 1908. Summers were spent in Milford, Pennsylvania where he led the Yale Forest School Camp.

Thornton Munger's sister, Eleanor, went on to marry Philip P. Wells who served as "Law Officer" for the U.S. Forest Service between 1907 and 1910. In an account of his work sent to Pinchot in 1913, Wells describes the "legal and administrative questions affecting the conservation of natural resources" after public lands were transferred from the General Land Office, part of the Interior Department, to the Forest Service under the Department of Agriculture.[1]

Through Munger's narrative, we learn of the challenges facing a young man growing up while seizing the rungs of opportu-

---

1 Philip P. Wells, "Philip P. Wells in the Forest Service Law Office," Forest History Newsletter 16, No. 1 (1972) : 22-29. https://foresthistory.org/wp-content/uploads/2017/01/wells.pdf

nity. In his own words, Munger describes how his classmates start west to romantic-sounding assignments while he goes to work in the Atlantic Building under an electric fan. In August, 1908, Munger was transferred to Oregon where he was assigned to study lodgepole pine at the newly created Regional office in Portland. In 1924, he was appointed first Director of the North-west Forest Experiment Station. He retired from the U.S. Forest Service in 1946.

Whether describing the office or the high prairie, Munger is filled with gratitude for the experience and skills gained in the Forest Service. In his narrative, he praises the Agency for its emphasis on science: "It is an evidence of vision, progressivism, and scientific spirit of the Forest Service that even under pressure to take over the administration of a tremendous acreage of almost unknown and undeveloped public forests with a ridiculously small crew of very young men, research was not neglected." Coincident with the pressing problems of manning, developing, and protecting the national forests, studies were carried on of growth and yield, silvical characteristics of the important species, and methods of reforestation.

At the end of his 15-page narrative, Munger recalls a dramatic scene at his sister's house on the fateful night of Pinchot's dismissal. Like so many young men and women who were drawn to forest conservation thanks to Gifford Pinchot, Munger was crestfallen. But that night and in the days that followed, the indefatigable Pinchot put on his best face reassuring those present that his dismissal was a mere flickering of the candle. He knew "the fight was on."

In 1939, the Society of American Foresters formed a committee to oversee the continued inventory and collection of Old Timer narratives. The committee was composed of Pinchot himself, Earle H. Frothingham, and Thornton T. Munger.

At 20 years old, I worked at the Marine Systems Laboratory, lodged deep in the concrete caverns of the American Museum of Natural History, a division of the Smithsonian Institution in Washington, D.C.. The lab was chaotic but led by a principled and charismatic leader as driven as Gifford Pinchot who hired me as a stenographer-typist to help fulfill a mission: the research and development of aquaculture projects off the Maine coast. I was first set to work in the office and then sent out to the field where I served as a cook aboard a research vessel, the Marsys Resolute. I was finding my way in life surrounded by marine biologists the way the eager Bertha Adams was surrounded by foresters.

When I had a few minutes to spare, I wandered down the hall where a solitary paleobotanist reigned over a collection of specimens from all over the world. Along with his collection of specimens, he was in charge of an SEM, a scanning electron microscope. The paleobotanist and I became friends and when I would appear, he would put down whatever he was doing and lead me through the long corridors of the Smithsonian where tall grey flat files housed the bones of birds, dinosaurs, and varieties of seeds he had collected from the guts of squirrels and mice at places like Pompeii and Mauna Loa. Other times, he let me peer through the lens of the microscope where I gazed upon the intricate patterns of life. We didn't know then what we know now about DNA and the extinction of species.

Work at the Smithsonian gave me an early sense of wonder. I was grateful that our nation had taken the time to support this effort, and had safeguarded the seeds of hope. Like so many of the Old Timers, I'd been exposed to exciting ideas at an early age, ideas that created a sense of reverence for nature and beauty, ideas about our capacity to change the world around us, and how science might support the restoration of ecosystems.

U.S. DEPARTMENT OF AGRICULTURE
FOREST SERVICE
PACIFIC NORTHWEST FOREST AND RANGE EXPERIMENT STATION

424 U.S. Court House,
Main and Sixth Streets,
Portland, Oregon,

January 8, 1940.

Mr. Gifford Pinchot,
1615 Rhode Island Ave., N.W.,
Washington, D.C.

My dear G.P.:

I was pleased to receive your letter of December 11 and to hear of your progress in writing the history of the conservation movement. I shall be glad to do my part toward preserving the history of the early days. However, my connection came a little late for the most dramatic days, and being confined at the start to silvical studies I did not get the first hand contact with public relations problems and the legal complications that confronted those in executive positions who were putting the national forests under administration.

I plan to take a few days off this winter to dig out my old diaries and put down what I think will be significant. In addition, I am going to take up the project with some of the older men who can contribute even more than I, like Tom Sherrard, E.T. Allen, C.S. Chapman, and Fred Ames.

May the best of success attend you in this useful undertaking. With best wishes for the new year.

Cordially yours,

Thornton T. Munger

1615 Rhode Island Ave., N.W.,
Washington, D.C.,
January 15, 1940.

Mr. Thornton T. Munger,
U.S. Forest Service,
424 U.S. Court House,
Main and Sixth Streets,
Portland, Oregon.

Dear Thornton:

Best thanks for yours of January 8.

I am delighted you are going to write

your story; and the more you can stir up

others of the old timers, the better.

Some of them gave me their accounts of

1911 and '12.

Every good wish,

Yours as always,

GP

THORNTON MUNGER
2755 BUENA VISTA DRIVE
PORTLAND, OREGON

October 1, 1940

Mr. Gifford Pinchot,
    1615 Rhode Island Ave. N.W.,
      Washington, D.C.

My dear Mr. Pinchot:

    I have been very tardy in complying with my
promise of January 8 to send you a narrative of my
connection with the early days of forestry. I have at last
prepared a few pages which cover the period until January
7, 1910. I enclose two copies of it thinking that one might
be put with the files of the Historical Committee of the
Society of American Foresters with whom you are working.

    I trust this is not too late to have some interest
for you in connection with your task of writing a history
of the forest conservation movement. I have had lots of
fun at odd moments reading over old diaries and some old
letters which my sister Rose has preserved. Someday I might
write the next chapter, noticing on rereading your letter
that you are interested in the epoch up until the War.

    I have urged a number of the old-timers to write
up their stories, men like E.T. Allen, Tom Sherrard, and
Fred Ames who would have much to record, but none of them,
so far as I know have yet sent you anything; I shall keep
after them.

May the best success attend you in completing the history which we are all looking forward to having.

Cordially yours,

Thornton T. Munger

⌒

MEMORANDUM FOR MR. GIFFORD PINCHOT

MY CONNECTION WITH THE EARLY DAYS OF FORESTRY

By

Thornton T. Munger

The first suggestion that I should choose forestry as a profession came to me from my sister Eleanor (Mrs. Philip P. Wells), when I was a freshman at Yale College. She said, "Why don't you take up this new thing, forestry, that Gifford Pinchot is starting. You like the out-of-doors and he says the country needs foresters and it is a fine life for a young man." The Yale Forest School, founded by the Pinchot family the year before, was only a few blocks from my home. It was attracting much attention as a new field of activity and with a natural bent toward studying and collecting flowers, and a love of outdoor life it was natural that I should take her suggestion to heart.

So in the summer of 1902 I attended the eight
weeks course in forestry given by the Yale Forest School
on the Pinchot Estate near Milford, Pennsylvania. Field
excursions and lectures by James W. Toumey and Walter
Mulford and campfire talks by such visitors as Gifford
Pinchot, Overton W. Price, George Sudworth, George
Schwartz, and F.L. Olmsted, whetted my enthusiasm for
forestry and convinced me that this was the career for me.

So the next summer I applied for employment in the
Bureau of Forestry, and was given a position as a Student
Assistant at a wage of twenty-five dollars a month. I was
assigned to a party, all youngsters, making a study of
white birch and poplar in Maine under Blaine S. Viles
and Jack Appleton. I counted rings, made stem analyses,
learned woodmanship under our French Canadian ax man,
and got my first real taste of primitive life in the Maine
wilderness and liked it.

The next summer (1904) as manager of the Yale
Forest School Camp at Milford, Pennsylvania. I gained
some of the executive experience a forester needs and saw
the Class of 1906 start on their first term in the forest
school. I shared their campfires and gained an increased
interest and knowledge of forestry as a career.

Though intending to enter the forest school
in the summer of 1905, a chance came to me to go abroad
and Professor Toumey and Dean Graves encouraged me to
take it, observe European forestry, and enter the forest
school the next year. So with letters of introduction

from Dean Graves and others, I sailed July 1, and had nine months in Western Europe, three of which were spent in visiting Southern German, Swiss, and Austrian forests and foresters.

Yale Forest School Camp, Milford, Pa, 1912

Photo courtesy Gerald W. Williams Collection, Oregon State University.

On my return I was employed by the forest school as foreman or handy man to put the Milford camp in shape for the summer session. Here I got my first experience in a very small way with road building, planting, and camp construction.

In early July of 1906 the class of 1908 gathered at Milford, nearly forty in number, the largest class of forestry students, I believe, ever assembled in this country up to that time.

In the two years of the forest school, hours were forgotten. There was keen zest to learn all about this new field. The call of the country for service and the lure of the West whetted our enthusiasm. Employment on graduation seemed assured. The spring term of senior year was spent in camp in Alabama where under Professor Chapman and Bryant, most practical work was given in the big logging woods and mills to clinch the previous theoretical training. In April the Civil Service examination for Forest Assistant was given especially for the benefit of the group at Sylacauga, Alabama. Twenty-eight Yale men took the exam, which in my case, involved writing 29 foolscap pages during the first of two seven-hour sessions. The returns showed that all the Yale men passed. Altogether 55 qualified out of the 99 who took the examination.

On July 1, 1908 I reported for duty as a Forest Assistant in Washington at a salary of $83.33 (sometimes $83.34) per month. It had been my expectation to be sent at once to the West to have a part in putting the national forests under technical administration. That was then the big task of the Forest Service, begun three years before when the Forest Reserves were transferred from the Department of the Interior. But when I got to Washington Mr. Rafael Zon, then Chief of the Office of Silvics—the research section of the Forest Service—urged me to accept assignment to that section, with the understanding that if I didn't like it I could change to administrative work. It seems that Mr. Zon had first choice in the selection of men from the Civil Service register. So I joined the office of Silvics, saw my classmates start west to romantic-sounding assignments, and went to work in the Atlantic Building under an electric fan.

It is an evidence of vision, progressiveness, and scientific spirit of the Forest Service that even under the pressure to take over the administration of a tremendous acreage of almost unknown and undeveloped public forests with a ridiculously small crew of very young men, research was not neglected. Coincident with the pressing problems of manning, developing, and protecting the national forests, studies were carried on of growth and yield, silvical characteristics of the important species, and methods of reforestation.

My first job was to write instructions for a cooperative study of phenology,[2] a subject entirely new to me until I searched the literature. Next I was given to rewrite for publication a short manuscript on Giant Arborvitae—a tree I had never seen. Then came a 135-page manuscript on loblolly pine for me—who had had mighty little experience with this tree—to put in shape for a bulletin. The courage of the Forest Service and of its young personnel in tackling jobs of all magnitude and degrees of complexity is quite amazing. And it is still more amazing that throughout the Service most jobs were accomplished acceptably.

I was selected to make a silvical study of the ashes and two weeks were spent in preparation for this. Then a

---

2 Phenology : The study of cyclic and seasonal natural phenomena, especially in relation to climate and plant and animal life. Oxford Dictionary.

shift in plans sent me the latter part of August to Oregon
to make a study of the encroachment of lodgepole pine on
western yellow pine in central Oregon.

In Portland I reported at the Forest Service
office which was then manned by Chief Inspector E.T.
Allen, three assistant inspectors, and a clerk. It was
news then when a forester came to Oregon and the *Oregon
Journal* carried the headlines "Expert to Spend Months
in Deschutes Reserve." The article quoted me as saying,
in regard to the competition between lodgepole pine
(a very low-value species) and western yellow pine (a
highly desirable species): "The government expects to
find some way to improve conditions by cutting the trees
in a different manner. Of course it will take a long time
to bring about the change, say 50 or 100 years, but Uncle
Sam is in the forestry business for all time to come and
he has become accustomed to looking a long way ahead."
This well illustrates the progressiveness and courage,
almost audacity, of the Forest Service of 1908 in sending
a 25-year-old easterner to study alone a highly complex
silvical problem in the primitive wilds of the West, any
practical remedy for which seemed very remote.

My journey to the theatre of conflict between
lodgepole and western yellow pine was accomplished by
train to Shaniko, then night 4-horse stage to Prineville,
64 miles in 13½ hours, and then, after a day at the
Supervisor's headquarters with Inspector Kent, another
horse stage trip of 67 miles in 15 hours to the hamlet of
Rosland. This consisted of a store, hotel, stage and feed
stables, ranger's 2-room house and office (the former

saloon), and a couple of residences, but was the biggest
town in 10,000 square miles. In a letter written August 30,
1908 I said: "It is a hotbed of land squabbles, however, and
the air is full of them. The Forest Service is more talked
of than any other subject, and though the people are very
polite, some of them are awfully sore at the Service. Many
of them have gotten claims fraudulently and got caught
by the Service or are trying to get timber land and claim
that it is agricultural. Nearly everybody who passes
through the town is looking for a place to locate...."
The same letter mentions a horseback ride with a land
promoter who "was anxious to show me about and pour a lot
of the home-seekers troubles in my ear so as to get on the
right side of the Forest Service, and I was glad to avail
myself of his local knowledge, though the land business is
none of my concern."

As an instance of my first impression of the
rangers whom I met--since confirmed by my experience
everywhere, or almost everywhere--I quote: "He (a ranger
from the Cascade National Forest) seems to be a dandy;
as are all the rangers I have met, men of fine character
and personality and of no mean administrative ability
combined with their physical and local capability."

Nearly three months were spent reconnoitering
the country from Bend to Klamath Falls, counting tree
reproduction, taking soil samples, studying from
horseback the distribution of the forest types, the
competition between lodgepole pine and western yellow
pine, and the succession of species after fires. Often
the local ranger or guard and I traveled together with

pack train, combining our work, fighting such fires
as were encountered, mapping recent burns for report
purposes, looking up administrative sites, and attending
to small timber sales or free use business. A mention
of my attending to a certain forest fire sounds rather
casual in comparison to present-day high speed methods
of detection, transportation, and suppression. The fire
had been burning for some time two miles from Crescent
when I ran across it on Wednesday. On Thursday afternoon
thinking that a light rain would have put the fire in
just the condition I wanted it, I got a shovel and went
around all the advancing burning line and fixed all the
dangerous places by removing the logs and needles and
throwing sand on the vigorous fires and in three or four
hours had it in such shape that it will cause no more
trouble, I think. The nearest ranger is 21 miles from here,
so I felt authorized to take time off from silvical work.

At the crossroads at Crescent, where I spent
a month in the only house, was a signboard which
illustrates the isolation of this central Oregon forest
at this time; with arrows pointing north, east, south, and
west, it read--

> "Prineville 84 miles
> Silver Lake 45 miles
> Klamath Falls 100 miles
> Eugene 115 miles"

September, October, and November 1908 were spent
in this silvical reconnaissance, scouring the country
along the east slope of the Cascade Range, riding often 20
and 30 miles daily, or walking all day when the country
was unsuitable for horse work or my horse needed a rest.

Then word came that I was to be assigned as
Chief of the Section of Silvics—a one-man section—
in the newly created district office to be established
in Portland. December 1 was the date set for this epoch
making decentralization of the Forest Service, by which
district offices were set up in six western cities. In
each was to be a Section of Silvics as part of the Branch
of Silviculture, evidencing that research was to have an
integral part in this decentralized management of the
national forests.

I was then told there was to be an experimental
forest located on one of the national forests of this
District, where I would probably make my headquarters.
But it was some years before District Six established an
experimental forest as such.

The first week of December 1908 a migration
of men and women arrived in Portland by transfer from
the Washington, D.C. office, established their homes
in this new city, and in an incredibly short time had a
37-room office of the Forest Service running smoothly
as the direct administrator of the national forests of
Oregon, Washington, and Alaska and as the focal center
for forestry education and research. E.T. Allen was

District Forester and Fred Ames as Chief of the Office of
Silviculture was my immediate boss.

The winter of 1908-9 saw the new district
organization get into smooth running condition, the
administration of the national forests was made more
direct and by close contact with the public some of the
dislike and mistrust of the Forest Service was allayed. As
a part of my job I organized and catalogued a library as a
necessary foundation for any technical work. Inquiries
from the public were answered often from very slim
knowledge, but without grievous mistakes, as I recall.
My first field trip into the Douglas-fir region was made
that winter in response to a request to explain the dying
of some timber. I attributed the trouble to bark beetles,
and in spite of my newness to the region, my forest school
course in entomology stood me in good stead and I believe
I was correct and that the inquirer was satisfied. When
spring opened I started on a month's circuit of central,
southern, and western Oregon. The technical jobs I did
on that trip were typical of pioneering research then
attempted.

(a) Examination of some "dying" timber on the Umatilla
     National Forest.

(b) Direct seeding experiments on the denuded lodgepole
     pine lands near Rosland.

(c)   Establishing a little experimental nursery, 18 x 12 feet, in which to try to grow some yellow pine seedlings. To stock this nursery 1,700 wild seedlings were dug up and packed on saddle horse four miles.

(d)   Laying out a pair of experimental plots in a timber sale area to test the relative merits of burning and not burning the brush.

(e)   Examine exotic trees planted in irrigated desert areas.

(f)   Stop at seven supervisors' offices to confer with supervisors and rangers and make plans for silvical studies.

In the course of this trip I rode 400 miles in horse stages--one stretch of which was from Silver Lake to Lakeview in 22 hours, and rode on eight different saddle horses.

It was decided that the major project for this first season of the new Section of Silvics would be a study of growth and yield of Douglas-fir. Nothing was known about this most important species, no volume tables were available, the location suitable for study had to be ferreted out. Part of the spring was taken up with making plans and interviewing timbermen. A visit to Seattle in May (1909) gave me a peek at the Alaska-Yukon Exposition

before it was open with Mr. Sudworth who was there
installing the Forest Service exhibit.

Professor E.G. Miller, Dean of the newly created
School of Forestry at the University of Washington, was
engaged for the summer to act as chief of one crew of two
student assistants while I took another crew of two.
For the first few days we worked together making tree
measurements and laying off sample plots in young stands.
Then he took the northern end of the Douglas-fir region
and I the southern.

We scoured the region on horseback, in wagons, on
logging train but mostly on foot, hunting for even-aged
immature stands suitable for our mensurational work.
We felled trees for tree analyses and measured sample
acres in stands of various ages all day and worked on our
notes in the evening--or sometimes when we were camping
fished for a mess of trout. We moved often, and boarded at
farmhouses, logging camps, or country hotels, frequently
putting up our tent when sleeping quarters were not
available inside. A walk of three or four miles to work was
thought nothing of, and 25 miles a day were not unusual
when I was scouting.

The work that summer was largely on private lands
in the foothills outside the national forest for there
could best be found the second-growth stands we wanted to
study and the logging operations where there were felled
trees to analyze.

Fire fighting then had the right of way over
all other work, but the facilities for coping with the

problem were scant in proportion with those of today.
When I discovered by chance a 160-acre fire on the Umpqua
National Forest in a bad brushy mountain side I walked
15 miles (round trip) to notify the ranger (who was not
at home). Next day our crew of three went to work on the
fire, the ranger rode 20 miles to get to it and together
we surrounded it with a fire line. In the evening I rode
horseback several miles to inform the state fire warden of
this fire that was on railroad land under his protection.
Then to sleep in the hay in a barn to the tune of cowbells,
goat bells, sheep bells and horses munching their hay,
wishing after these two extra-strenuous days--as my
letter of September 3, 1909 states--that Senator Heyburn
could be with me even for part of a day to disprove his
statement that 'Forest Officers sit around hotel verandas
in their gay green uniforms all summer."

Field work on the Douglas-fir growth and yield
study stopped early in October when the student assistants
had to return to college. Office work on this study
occupied much of the next few months, for volume tables as
well as growth and yield tables had to be compiled by Miss
Bell, the computing clerk, and myself from the data six of
us had collected during a long summer. I rented an adding
machine, then considered quite a novelty, and wrote to the
Washington office for permission to buy one.

But for this one-man research section there were
many other jobs to be done both in field and office. Among
the short field trips that fall was one on the Oregon
National Forest to install an experiment in direct
seeding. There being no nursery stock available, there was

hope that artificial seeding of old burns, even of exotic
conifers and hardwoods, might be successful. After a day's
trip in from Portland by train, stage, and horseback and
making camp in a one room log cabin near the planting site
it began to snow. The next morning there was six inches
of snow on the ground, and our six horses looked forlorn
and hungry. The local forest officers and I set to work
planting our seed in spots, but the snow soon got too deep
for that and we hurriedly broadcasted the pine, maple and
chestnut seeds we had left, packed up, and left before we
were trapped in there by too deep snows, and it was late at
night before we got to a cabin and pasture below the snow
line and in the rain belt.

Another trip was made to the Wind River valley,
Columbia National Forest, to study the reproduction on
the logged-off land of one of the first, if not the first,
national forest timber sale of any consequences in the
Douglas-fir region. I stayed in the farm house of the old-
time ranger, who typified the transition from a pioneer
frontiersman to a government land manager. I wrote of him
(October 31, 1909): "When he started in here a few years ago
the settlers were all dead against the Forest Service and
Reserves, took no precautions against fires, and generally
mistrusted the government work. Now the people are all
behind the Forest Service, they believe the reserves
are good things, there are no more forest fires due to
carelessness, and this big 30,000,000 foot sale of timber
is going along as smooth as possible with no friction
between buyer and government." This contemporary comment
on the Forest Service's place in public opinion is perhaps

overly optimistic, viewed in retrospect, but it indicates
the rapid change that came following the establishment
of the district offices with more direct local contact
between Forest Service men and the people.

My letters to my family in New Haven made
occasional mention of the public's attitude toward the
Forest Service. For example on July 19, 1909, I wrote,
"One sees his (Pinchot's) name more than that of almost any
other public man, except Taft, in these western papers
and not entirely in a friendly connection. The *Portland
"Oregonian"* is trying to keep alive the Pinchot-Ballinger
disagreement[2] and sides wholly against Pinchot. But there
is a great deal of friendly feeling toward the Forest
Service from all sides and most of the complaints come
from disgruntled grafters, whom the Forest Service has
very rightly opposed." Again on August 15, 1909: "Did you
read about the fine reception that Pinchot got at Spokane?
I wish that he would get that warm a one in Portland and
Seattle."

I went East at Christmas time 1909 to visit
my family in New Haven and after New Years went to
Washington to be with my sister, Mrs. Wells, and her
family. Her husband, Philip P. Wells, was a classmate of
Gifford Pinchot and on the evening of January 7, 1910
while I was visiting at my brother-in-law's house he

---

[2]   Also referred to as the Pinchot-Ballinger Affair, this bitter conflict embodied conflicting approaches to the conservation of natural resources.

was invited to dine informally with the family and close friends, Mrs. and Miss Parris. Mr. Pinchot came a few minutes late and explained that on leaving his house he had been handed two letters by the White House messenger, which he had stopped to read hurriedly by a street lamp. At the dinner table he read aloud these letters—the not-unexpected letters from President Taft and Secretary Wilson dismissing him from his position as Chief of the Forest Service. It was a dramatic hour, seeming tragic to those who had lost their leader in the fight for forest conservation, but to him only a further call that the fight was on. It was clear to us at that table that he did not feel this blow on himself; he only feared what it might mean to his associates and the Service. So ends the era of Pinchot's actual administration of the Forest Service, but his influence continues to be felt through the warp and woof of the organization. Policies and procedures he so wisely founded continue to vitalize the Forest Service; the form and language to be used in correspondence, the policy of decentralized administration, the spirit of public service that pervades the personnel, the principle of conservation through use, the concept that a research unit is a necessity for progressive administration.

These were the formative years of the Forest Service—the Pinchot era—in which I am very glad my connection with the forestry movement began.

THORNTON T. MUNGER

September 22, 1940

1615 Rhode Island Ave., N.W.,
Washington, D.C.,
October 22, 1940.

Mr. Thornton T. Munger,
2755 Buena Vista Drive,
Portland, Oregon.

Dear Thornton:

I am ashamed of myself for my
long delay in thanking you for your admirable
story. I have read it with the keenest
interest--every word of it, and I am immensely
obliged to you for giving me one of the very
best accounts I have had.

With every good wish,

Yours as always,

GP

GP:AMB

Mr. Pinchot had to leave
town before he could sign.

chapter 10

Agnes V. Scannell
WASHINGTON D.C., REGION 6
(PORTLAND) ALASKA
1907–1918

"But that was the spirit pervading the whole Forest Service. Cooperation everywhere; encouragement everywhere; courtesy everywhere. The higher officials always wanted to make those in lesser stations feel that they were just as important; there was no distinction because of classification; all were working for one purpose, for one cause—the Forests of America!"

—Agnes V. Scannell

Agnes V. Scannell graduated from Worcester High School in Worcester, Massachusetts in 1901. She joined the Portland Regional Office of the U.S. Forest Service in 1907 before being posted to Washington, D.C. and Alaska. We do not know very much about Agnes Scannell except that she took advantage of every opportunity offered and felt indebted to the U.S. Forest Service for her success.

In her narrative, we find Agnes Scannell quite single-minded and always, as she put it, going forth. "Forth I went to Washington," she wrote. At another point, "Forth I went across this great and magnificent continent, whose expanse no one can visualize until it has been traversed..." Going forth was how she helped others. Going forth was how she lived her life. Gifford Pinchot and the U.S. Forest Service gave Agnes Scannell an opportunity to use her energy and enthusiasm. So, forth she went, crossing the country, boarding ships to Alaska, noticing the handsome foresters at work, and embracing every minute, full speed ahead.

Perhaps Agnes Scannell was a mystic. We learn from her narrative that she took clues from outside events such as losing her handbag on a westbound train. She was outgoing, a problem-solver, trusting a complete stranger on a train platform to help her. She was engaged in her quest for a better life, bound and determined to reach her destination.

There is an Agnes Scannell in each of us. Despite the odds and obstacles encountered each day, we are here to help one another. Looking back, Agnes Scannell knew why she'd been bold. She was young. "There was the opportunity to cross the Continent," she wrote. "I remember how I looked at the map daily, and drew my finger from Massachusetts to Oregon. Naturally, at times, a little faint-heartedness overtook me; I felt almost afraid to go. But I was young! I had the health, and strength, and ambition, imagination, and all the things that youth is heir to. We were all young! Almost everyone in the Forest Service was young. The Forest Service itself was young! And everywhere there seemed to be that vigor, that onward-push, that dauntless spirit that goes with youth."

Agnes Scannell's narrative takes us with her on an adventure, to the great Falls of Niagara, through the bitter cold of

St. Paul, Minnesota and through the Rockies. "They seem to give me courage," she wrote, "and I began to feel bolder and bigger too, under their spell."

AGNES V. SCANNELL
718 CAMBRIDGE STREET
BRIGHTON, MASSACHUSETTS

December 27, 1939.

Honorable Gifford Pinchot,
    1615 Rhode Island Avenue, N.W.,
      Washington, D.C.

My dear Mr. Pinchot:

    Your letter of December 11, 1939, came as an echo of the past. It was like the response to a thought- wave upon the ether. For just a year ago, on New Year's Day, 1938, while visiting my cousin, Florens Donoghue, Esq. of Worcester, Massachusetts, I mentioned to him that I had been hoping I should someday have an opportunity to put in writing some facts about the Forest Service of the United States, because I felt a written record should be made of the efforts of Gifford Pinchot in establishing this important branch of the Government.

    Both my cousin and his wife can confirm this. I tell it to you so you may understand how happy I was when I received your letter, asking me to write an account of my connection with the Forest work of the Government, and to narrate my experiences in my own way.

Since I served only as a young stenographer, I fear I may not be able to contribute information of much value. However, I am glad to send you, herewith, a narrative of my experience with the Forest Service, from January, 1907, to October, 1918.

Believe me,

Very sincerely yours,

Agnes Veronica Scannell

Enclosures

Experiences of Agnes V. Scannell,
while stenographer with the United States Forest
Service, Washington D.C., and Portland, Oregon.
January 1907, to October, 1918.

Back in the year 1906, I spent the summer in Europe.
It was my first adventure away from the conservative
little city of Worcester, Massachusetts—the home of
Honorable George Frisbie Hoar, former United States
Senator; the late Rear-Admiral Earle, of the United States
Navy; and the late Arthur Prentice Rugg, Chief Justice of
the Supreme Court of Massachusetts. Those are only a few
of the many Worcester men who have served their country. I
mention them in order to show that at the beginning of the
twentieth century, the High School students of Worcester
could acquaint themselves with the lives of such men,
whose achievements were inspirations to aspire. It was
only natural, then, that the members of the graduating
class of 1901, should hope to be of some service to their
country.

Gaining courage and ambition from my European trip,
I returned home eager to go beyond the confines of my
little city; and so in October, 1906, I took a Civil Service
examination at Boston, for the Departmental Service.
In December, 1906, I received an appointment to the
Forest Service, at Washington, D.C. It was just before the
Christmas holidays, and I accepted the appointment with

the understanding that I should not report for duty until January 2, 1907.

Forth I went to Washington, and reported for duty to the Forest Service, then located in an old rented building on "F" Street, N.W. I shall have to admit that I was at first taken back, for I had seen views of the many beautiful Government buildings shown in a *National Geographic Magazine,* and I pictured myself working in one of those buildings. The Forest Service was a branch of the Department of Agriculture, and other branches within that Department were spaciously housed in Government buildings, placed on spacious lots of land. Since I always liked space and a beautiful view, my early inquiries were directed, for the most part, as to why we were so crowded in our poor quarters. The response from my fellow workers was always the same, namely that the Forest Service appropriation was very small, and that was the best we could expect. I was soon to learn that the Congressional appropriations for the Forest Service were small indeed, and although the Service was expanding in leaps and bounds, the appropriations appeared to be contracting in the same ratio.

My appointment read: "Clerk, stenographer, typewriter, at six hundred dollars per annum." That was fifty dollars a month, which was to cover my added living expenses, since I was away from home, as well as all other maintenance; there was, of course, little of my salary left at the end

of the month. But money was not my objective—experience
was. And how fortunate I was to have those early
experiences come to me in the Forest Service!

My first assignment was in a crowded room, where
all new appointees were placed, in order to try out their
abilities and aptitudes. A young woman, whose name I have
forgotten, was our supervisor. I shall never forget her
graciousness and guidance. After a few weeks under her
observation, I was assigned to Mr. Rowden's department.
Here I was trained in the minutest details of Forest
Service procedure, relating to correspondence, filing,
and the care and distribution of Department papers.
It was here I began to sense the perfect organization,
the splendid cooperation, and the remarkable courtesy
all around me, as well as the excellent training I was
receiving. Then the offensiveness of the congested
quarters began to disappear from my consciousness.

I am really at a loss to know how to describe the
training each new appointee received before being given
a definite assignment. No detail was overlooked; and
when one had passed through that training, he or she
might forevermore measure up to the highest standard of
secretarial efficiency, and that included the ability to
set up letters in correct and artistic style; to couch or
phrase a letter concisely and with dignity; to preserve
and distribute carbon copies, so carefully initialed, that
without the loss of a second, the one who dictated, the

secretary who wrote, and the recipient of any paper could be identified. I can truthfully say that my training in the Forest Service served as the cornerstone for my success in later years, irrespective of the fields of endeavor into which I have entered; and they have been many and varied.

In the year 1917, when I returned to Washington, D.C., because of the World War, I met a former Forest Service employee, a Miss Nellie Dillon of the Denver District. Upon learning that I, too, had been in the Service, one of her first remarks was "Haven't you found that the training you received in the Forest Service filled all your needs, and was a foundation for your later successes?" How interested I was to learn that what had been my personal experience had also been hers! And in 1918, when I renewed my acquaintance with Miss Pearl Schroeder, a former co-worker in the Service at Portland, Oregon, and who was then in some other branch of the Government at Washington, she passed a similar remark.

So much for the training that every Forest Service secretary received. What a splendid system that was! No delays because of blunders on the part of new stenographers; no running about, looking for papers; no lost or mislaid papers; everything moving with efficiency and dispatch.

Eventually, I was assigned to the office of "Boundaries." In the Service, each department had its appropriate name. Here every desk was jammed against the other, with barely enough room to move about, and I wrote

all day about the southeast Quarter of Section so-and-so;
the Northwest Quarter of Section thus-and-thus, in
Township such-and-such. The work had little meaning
for me, and I found it rather monotonous. By June, 1907,
there was a rumor that the Washington Office was about to
be decentralized and Districts established in the west.
In July, definite statements were issued, and a call for
volunteers was made, for men and women trained in the
Washington Office, who would be willing to go to the newly
established districts in the west, where their training
would be needed. There were to be six districts as follows:

Denver, Colorado	Albuquerque, New Mexico
Missoula, Montana	San Francisco, California
Ogden, Utah	Portland, Oregon

At the time some one wrote a poem entitled 'The
Hegira" my copy of which I have often wished I had kept. It
began somewhat like this:

> " Oh, they're whispering in the offices,
> And they're talking in the hall,
> For everyone is wondering
> Where to migrate in the Fall."

Each one could make his own choice, up to the time
when all positions would be filled. I remember there was
a great clamor for Denver, since that was the nearest
station; so I put my bid in for Denver, on time. However, in

August, I returned to Worcester for my vacation, and while
there sought advice about western migration. I talked
first with my brother Joseph, who had become my devoted
counsellor after my mother's death. He gave his consent to
my going, with the remark:

> "Worcester will always be here when you want to
> return; but the opportunity to go west will not
> always be here."

Regarding the choice of station, I talked with
the late Honorable Rufus B. Dodge, who had been a
personal friend of my mother. I shall always remember
that interview. He thought the opportunity to go west
a splendid one, and he advised me to select Portland,
Oregon. I can see him, even now, as he tipped back in his
office chair, while he remarked, "that wonderful Pacific
Slope." Taking his advice, upon my return to Washington,
I immediately sought to change my choice of station, and
asked for assignment to Portland. I was told I might have
it, for few wished to go there, because of the distance,
while there was a waiting list for Denver.

To those who volunteered to go west, a promotion of
three hundred dollars per annum was given, as well as all
expenses paid to the western post. That meant an increase
of salary to $900, and it seemed like a big sum in those
days. Besides, there was the opportunity to cross the
continent. I remember how I looked at the map daily, and

drew my finger from Massachusetts to Oregon. Naturally,
at times, a little faint-heartedness overtook me; I felt
almost afraid to go. But I was young! I had the health,
and strength, ambition, imagination, and all things that
youth is heir to. We were all young! Almost everyone in the
Forest Service was young. The Forest Service itself was
young! And everywhere there seemed to be that vigor, that
onward-push, that dauntless spirit that goes with youth.

But youth is prone to overlook the sense
of responsibility and feeling of concern which
unquestionably was gripping the minds of the more mature
officials of the Service. For to scatter hundreds of young
men and women throughout the great west, far from home
and kindred, must have caused considerable anxiety to
those who were guiding the destinies of this young branch
of the Government. It was at this time I began to learn more
about the Forest Service, its beginnings and its purpose. I
made inquiries, and here is what I was told:

> The Forest service was established during the
> administration of President Theodore Roosevelt.
> In establishing this new branch of the Government
> President Roosevelt acted upon the advice of Mr.
> Gifford Pinchot, who was a member of a wealthy and
> aristocratic family of French Huguenot extraction.
> The family had been engaged in the making of wall
> papers, and this industry necessarily brought them
> into contact with lumbermen and forests. Mr. Gifford
> Pinchot soon became aware that if the ruthless
> cutting of timber continued, with no attempt to

reforest, within a few decades the United States
would suffer from a timber famine.

Unlike most people at the time, who were
engaged in industries which used forest products,
Mr. Pinchot looked beyond the needs of his own
business into the vital interests of his country,
and felt a grave concern at forest conditions. That
is why he appealed to President Roosevelt, who was
his personal friend, and urged the withdrawal of
forested public lands in the west, so they might be
set apart as Forest Reserves.

Thus it was in the mind and heart of Gifford Pinchot
that the Forest Service was conceived. That is the story
as it was told to me. I accepted it, and have ever since
believed it.

Today, it would be difficult to think of America
without Forest Reserves; it would seem incredible; and
yet that could be the case, were it not for the idealism
of the Pinchots. In the year 1906, conservation was a new
concept in American national life; few there were who
really grasped the connotation of the word. It became a
familiar, everyday word to me in the Forest Service. It
was conservation which saved America from a threatened
timber famine that was coming so swiftly, had it not been
halted by Gifford Pinchot's vision and his concern for
future generations, that its disastrous effects would have
shaken America.

Back in Washington, in the meantime, summer had
merged into autumn; autumn into winter; and the time was

drawing near for the "hegira." Just before Thanksgiving—
and Thanksgiving Day then was the old traditional
day, the last Thursday in November—I was given an
authorization to procure my ticket from Worcester,
Massachusetts, to Portland, Oregon, for I had permission
to spend the Thanksgiving holidays at home. I was to
report at Portland for duty on December 7, 1907. Forth I
went across this great and magnificent continent, whose
expanse no one can visualize until it has been traversed,
and fearing I might want to turn back somewhere along the
route, I carried with me enough money to pay my return
expenses even from the Pacific Coast.

Just before reaching Buffalo, New York, some agent
boarded the train to sell tickets for a trip to Niagara
Falls, and I became so engrossed in the purchase of the
ticket, that when I alighted from the train I realized I
had left my pocketbook behind. However, I did not become
alarmed, for there was only ten dollars in it, and my
ticket for Oregon. My mother had taught me to always carry
large sums of money on my person, so my return fare was
safely hung about my neck in a little bag. In those days
high-necked dresses were the style, so anything might be
hung around a woman's neck, unnoticed. When I discovered
my thoughtlessness, I made a little exclamation, and
standing near by, was a gentleman who heard me and
promptly asked if he could help me. I told him what had
happened, and in an instant he was off looking for the

station master, who telephoned to some tower a short
distance away, where the train was signaled to stop, so
that my pocketbook might be recovered. Luckily I was able
to give the name of my Pullman car, having made a mental
note of it as I stepped on. As I sat waiting in the station
for results, I began to think that perhaps it all happened
for the best, and that if the pocketbook was not returned,
then I should take that as a sign that I was to turn back,
when in walked a trainman, swinging my little pocketbook;
then I knew that was the signal for me to go on.

I spent the day at Niagara. It was the first time I had
seen the Falls, and what a spectacle! There had been an ice
storm and everything about the Falls, the surrounding
rocks, and all the trees, had become crystallized,
as it were. It was like a fairy land, unimaginable,
indescribable. It was very cold, so after viewing the
beauty of the Falls and their surroundings, I spent the
remainder of the time in the cozy, warm library, where I
read the first book my hand touched—"Old Lavender and
Lace." The train for the west was due about five o'clock,
and I "went on board" until my next stop the following
morning— Chicago, where I was to be met by my cousins
with whom I had spent the summer of 1906 in Europe, and
with whom I looked forward to having a pleasant reunion
at their home.

The first stop beyond Chicago was St. Paul, Minnesota,
where again I almost turned back, for it was bitter, bitter

cold, and I had to wait there four hours for the train, which was to take me to the Coast. On, on, I went, however, and the trip over the Northern Pacific Lines I enjoyed very much. I was eager to see the Rockies. In Montana they are magnificent; so young; so bold; so high. They seemed to give me courage, and I began to feel bolder and bigger too, under their spell. Once I crossed the Great Divide, I realized I was standing alone in the vastness of the west; hence I must not waiver, for the "die was cast." The train reached Portland, Oregon, early in the morning of December 7, and I reported for duty about 9:30 o'clock, at the Beck Building, where were located the Forest Service offices of District 6.

The Beck Building was a new, modern one, well located in the center of Portland, and the offices were large and airy. The surroundings were a decided improvement over the crowded conditions at Washington. I was assigned to the branch called "Products." There were many branches, such as "Lands,""Silviculture,""Grazing," "Law," etc. My Chief was Mr. Joseph Knapp, a handsome young man from Indiana, who was a graduate of Purdue University. Within a few days another handsome young man reported for duty. He was Mr. Oakleaf, from Olean, New York and a graduate of Biltmore Forest School, I believe. I enclose herewith a picture of the Portland office of Products. Mr. Oakleaf is seated at his desk and I am seated at the typewriting desk. Mr. Oakleaf appears to be smoking his favorite little

pipe, while I appear to be taking dictation from him. We
were only posing for the picture, for Mr. Oakleaf would
never smoke while he was dictating. A little later on Mr.
Cox reported; he was a graduate of Yale Forest School, I
believe. So everyone came well trained for the work to be
done.

Agnes Scanell and Mr. Oakleaf.
From the narrative of Agnes V. Scannell. Library of Congress. Manuscript Division.
Gifford Pinchot Collection. Old Timers Collection.

I am going to digress right here for a minute, and
quote an excerpt from a little message I received just
yesterday--December 26, 1939--which came to me from Miss
Catherine Reed, who is still employed in the Portland
office of the Forest Service, now located in the Post Office

Building. All through the years we have remembered each
other with greetings during the Christmas season, and
along with her greeting this year came the following note:

"Dear friend Agnes: I hope you are well and happy
this Christmas. Mr. Knapp's son who has a high-class
position in Europe, married this past summer, and he and
his bride came to Portland on their honeymoon. They were
made quite a lot of, and their pictures appeared in one of
the newspapers....The young man is quite a handsome chap,
but not so much so as his dad, when he was the same age...."
I quote this in order to show that I am not exaggerating
when I refer to Mr. Knapp as handsome.

During the first week after my arrival in Portland,
I stayed at the Young Women's Christian Association. It
was their new quarters and I was made very comfortable.
However, I cannot forget the first evening of my arrival
in Portland. Upon going to my room at the "Young Women's"
I threw myself across the bed, and sobbed, "Oh, what have I
done! What have I done!"

I was seized with a terrible fear, when I thought of
the great expanse which separated me from my own. But
before long I was sound asleep, for there is something
about the air in Portland that puts new-comers to sleep; it
acts like an anaesthetic, until one becomes accustomed to
the ozone. So I slept soundly from five o'clock until nine
that evening, and when I awoke I retired for the night,
"without supper". In the morning I felt refreshed from the

sound sleep, and went to the office. As the day wore on, my
fears dimmed, so the next evening when I fell asleep, I did
so in a less distressed frame of mind.

Weeks passed, and having found a good home in
which to live, at number 35, 18th Street, corner of Couch,
Portland, I began to feel more at ease. I have been able to
put this address down, because all these years I have kept
a letter addressed to me there by the late reverend Francis
J. Tondorf, S.J., of Georgetown University. Who was he? On
January 23, 1920, the "New York World" printed a picture of
Father Tondorf, with the following caption:

"Father Tondorf of Georgetown University, to whom
everybody turns for information whenever there is an
earthquake."

I met this great scientist while in Washington,
and he frequently wrote to me in Oregon, because he was
interested in the progress of the Forest Service.

My official duties in the office of <u>Products</u> grew
more interesting every day. I always welcomed the
dictation periods, for I learned so much about the trees
of the "Northwest." That magnificent tree, scientifically
termed <u>pseudo pseudo taxifolia</u>[1] or <u>false hemlock,</u> and

---

1   The scientific name for the Douglas fir, referred to by Agnes Scannell as Pseudo
    pseudo taxifolia, has changed. Named for Scottish botanist David Duncan, the
    "Doug Fir" is now known as Pseudotsuga menziesii after another Scotsman,
    Archibald Menzies, surgeon and naturalist, who is reported to have been
    the first European to identify the tree in 1793 during the George Vancouver
    expedition. https://oregonencyclopedia.org/articles/douglas-fir

usually referred to as Douglas Fir was of most importance
and rightly so.

Timber preservation was another important subject;
the treatment of timber used for telegraph poles, or
piling in wharfs, with creosote or other preservatives in
order to repel insect attack and ward off decay. There were
many exhibits in the office showing treated and untreated
timber; one in particular I remember, a cross section of a
piece of piling which, because untreated, had been bored
through in numerous pieces by insects, until the pole
was practically eaten away inside. Such poles, or piling,
become dangerous as well as expensive, for they have to
be replaced at frequent intervals. Here again the Forest
Service rendered great service to the American public, for
by experiments conducted at Forest Service Laboratories,
it was proven that the length of life of timber could be
multiplied many times by having the timber treated with
preservatives. Literature was printed on this subject and
distributed free for the benefit of Americans. I recall
writing considerably about the "elastic limit," and saw
an experiment designed to show that limit; which is the
amount of strain a given piece of timber can stand before
smashing.

Considerable correspondence passed between the
Portland office and the various Ranger Stations within
National Forests; there was also much correspondence with
the Timber Testing Laboratory of the Forest Service at

the University of Wisconsin, Madison. The saving of the
forests from fires was always a matter of great concern,
and at certain seasons of each year, there came to us, edged
in black, a list of the names of those heroic men in the
Service who gave up their lives fighting fires.

Naturally, while working in such an atmosphere, one
could not help placing a great value upon trees. I began
to think of them as something almost human, for after all,
they are something alive, something growing, something
reproducing, something serving man. I have ever since
loved trees, and grieve to see them hurt, wounded or
killed. Many times since I have looked for a long time
at pictures of trees, particularly ones like "the fight
at timber line" depicting the terrific battle being
waged between the forces of ice, snow, and wind, and the
valiant tree, with its roots clutching to the thin earth
on the bleak mountain side. I like, too, that one entitled,
"the old guard dies, it never surrenders." Perhaps such
pictures appeal to me more now, as I approach the timber-
line of life. In these troubled times may I hold fast to
those roots embedded in Christian principles as the tree
clings to the mountain side. When at last there comes a
flash of Light to blind me from the dreaded chasm until it
is crossed, may I stand straight and strong like the tree
until it is torn asunder instantaneously by the bolt of
lightning.

During the summer of 1908, Miss Erma Bell of the
Portland Office and I took a trip to Mt. Hood, and en route
stopped for a few days at Adolph Aschoff's Mountain Home,
because near there was a ranger station, and both of us
wanted to see how Forest Rangers lived. Since the twilight
is long in Oregon, we started out early in the evening to
find the Ranger Station. As I look back at the experience
now, I shudder to think of the risk, for we might easily
have been lost in that forest on the slopes of the Cascades,
and overtaken by the blackness of night and the danger of
bears, we might not have returned. Fortunately, however,
we arrived at the Ranger's gate just as darkness began
to fall. The Ranger was on one of his inspection tours
of the forest, and his wife, a charming young woman,
welcomed us. In true Forest Service comradeship she made
us comfortable for the night. With her in that lonely spot
was only a dog—a very intelligent dog—named "I know",
and a little house-maid who might be described as just
having missed being classified as non compos mentis. The
Ranger's wife said no one else would accept a position in
that lonely, isolated place, and while of course the maid
lacked the qualification of companionship, nevertheless
she was a human being, and that meant something. The dog
was trained to go out to the creek and bring back a pail of
water. He also brought in the wood, stick by stick, in his
mouth. During the evening he entertained us with many
pranks, and later when we had gone up stairs to our room,

we heard the patter of feet; outside the door stood "I Know" with towels and soap in his mouth. The Ranger's wife told us that frequently she had to be alone thus for months at a time, having no contact with the outside world, except a telephone line which was connected only with the Portland Office. Sometime she accompanied her husband on his inspection tour of the forest, and lived for weeks in the saddle, dismounting only to cook the meals, and sleep upon blankets on the forest floor. At midnight we were startled by horses hoofs and a knock at the door. It was Mr. Aschoff's son who, fearing we might have become lost, rode through the blackness of the forest to inquire if we were safe. That was chivalry indeed!

Early the next morning as we walked back through the forest, there came to my mind the words of a song I had learned at school many years before. In the pure air of the rosy morning, in that beautiful forest, my soul was stirred, and with a strong, clear voice that rang through the trees, I sang to the forest:

> "O, vales with sunlight smiling,
> O, leafy woodland shades,
> What joy when morn is beaming
> To wander through your glades!
>
> The town and all its pleasures
> No charms for me disclose,
> But 'mid the sylvan forest
> My heart finds sweet repose

But 'mid the sylvan f-o-r-e-s-t
My heart--finds--sweet--repose."

Mr. Aschoff, Senior, saw us coming down the trail, and ran to meet us. Putting his arms around us, he said:

"Oh, I was afraid last night that a big bear had caught you!"

I believe it was during the fall of 1908 that Mr. Anderson visited the Portland Office. At Washington, for the young stenographers, Mr. Anderson typified discipline. I don't know why, for while there I had never seen him. But he seemed to be the one man everybody was afraid of, for he was supposed to be very exacting, and the standard of conduct and of the work had to be very high to pass Mr. Anderson's scrutinizing eye.

At Portland, he spent some time talking to Mr. Knapp, and then he addressed me. He spoke in a kindly, fatherly way, pointing out the finest and best in Forest Service work. Facing him for the first time, I stood silent and motionless, torn within between the emotions of fear, because of his reputation in Washington, and that of astonishment, at his gentle, kindly attitude towards me. I felt stronger and better after that interview.

Then, later, came our Chief, Mr. Gifford Pinchot. I remember that a little assembly was called in the evening; I can't think just where; and we were addressed by him. That was my first meeting with the Chief Forester, and he

shook hands with all of us. From that assembly I took away
two lasting impressions:

1.   The greatest of humility.

2.   The thought he asked us to take away.

What was that thought? We were to remember that we were
not working for him, only with him; we were all working
together for the forests of America.

I repeat "the greatness of his
Humility", for was not that the outstanding
characteristic of the Saviour? Is not that the
reason why children pray:

"Humble Jesus, meek and mild,"?

Still later on, came Mr. Hall from the Forest Service
at Madison, Wisconsin. He was on a general inspection
tour, and he dictated to me the observation he had made at
the District previously visited. The material was in the
form of a report for the Forester at Washington. Mr. Hall
left immediately for San Francisco, instructing me to
forward the report to him when I had transcribed my notes.
About ten days later, there came a letter from him, in
which he wrote:

"The report has been so well written it
will not have to be rewritten. I am sending it
directly to Washington."

Naturally I was very much elated, and my Chief, Mr. Knapp, having seen the letter first, was elated too.

But that was the spirit pervading the whole Forest Service. Cooperation everywhere; encouragement everywhere; courtesy everywhere. The higher officials always wanted to make those in lesser stations feel that they were just as important; there was no distinction because of classification; all were working for one purpose, for one cause—the Forests of America!

During the summer of 1909, the Alaska, Yukon, Pacific Exposition was held at Seattle, Washington. The Forest Service had a splendid exhibit at this Exposition, and it was there I witnessed the demonstration of the "elastic limit" of timber. Practically everyone in the Portland Office went to Seattle that summer. A group of secretaries who spent several days there, included Miss Pearl Schroeder, Miss Madsen, Miss Elsa Bernhardt, and Mrs. Riddell.

Miss Schroeder and I were en route to Alaska, to take the inland cruise, with Skagway as our destination. At Sitka, we met Mr. Fred Ames, and the Alaskan Supervisor, whose name I have forgotten. Mr. Ames was on official business from the Portland Office. The Forest Service launch *The Tongas* was at anchor, so Mr. Ames and the Supervisor invited us on board, where we were served tea by a Japanese male servant. I remember the Supervisor having shown us an Afghan that his mother had knitted for him, and he seemed very proud of it. As I write this, and recall those incidents, it seems to me that in those days people knew how to evaluate the worth-while things in life. The Alaskan Supervisor's post was an isolated one. During those weeks and months while he cruised up and down the bleak coast of Alaska, he must have had many lonely hours. Yet, I could observe that he was happy and enthusiastic about his work.

What was it.....what was it..... that made us all so happy in the Forest Service? What made us all so strong, physically, mentally, and spiritually, when we were separated from those we loved and from the solicitous care to be found only in one's home? I shall give the answer at the end of my narrative.

I enclose also, herewith, two views of THE TONGAS in Alaskan waters. In one picture Mr. Ames is plainly visible, standing on the bridge; in the other he may be seen, still standing on the bridge, but the launch is so close to Taku Glacier, that the Glacier stands out as the important thing in the picture. Here is also a view of Alaskan timber, taken about the same time.

Returning to Portland, the year 1910 soon rolled around, and with it came a cloud, the first cloud to envelop the Forest Service, and dim our spirits, which had basked in such bright sunlight. It was a nimbus cloud, presaging a storm, and it appeared suddenly in our firmament. Since we were so far from Washington, definite information could not be easily procured,

The Tongas in Alaskan waters.
From the narrative of Agnes V. Scannell. Library of Congress. Manuscript Division.
Gifford Pinchot Collection. Old Timers Collection.

as to what caused the trouble. I recall hearing that a
dispute had arisen about the rich coal lands of Alaska.
Mr. Pinchot, still concerned about the conservation of
America's natural resources, was urging the President,
William Howard Taft, to set aside those rich coal fields as
national reserves. However, pressure from other sources
was being brought upon President Taft, to make the coal
fields available to private capitalists. I remember
hearing the names of Ballinger and Guggenheim in this
connection. The result was the resignation of our Chief,
Gifford Pinchot.

Vividly do I recollect the excitement that spread
throughout the entire District Office. How each official
hastened to send a message! Our Chief must know that the
entire Forest Service stood solidly behind him, even

though it meant opposition to the viewpoint of President Taft. One telegram, sent by Mr. Fred Allen, I believe, who was District Supervisor at Portland, clearly demonstrated this. The telegram embodied a quotation from St. Paul's Epistle to the Colossians, Chapter 3, verse 25, and read as follows:

"They have sought to do you wrong. 'But he that doeth wrong shall receive for the wrong which he hath done: and there is no respect of persons.'"

Mr. Graves, formerly of the Yale Forest School, then became Chief Forester, but Mr. Pinchot continued to live in the memory of those who saw the Service grow great and strong under his guidance. Of course the work went forward, for that is what Mr. Pinchot would want, until today the Forest Service has expanded to immense proportions. But it can never surpass the greatness of the mind and heart of the man who built the Forest Service.

I shall now give the answer as to why, in the early years of the Service we all felt so strong, mentally and spiritually, and why our old Chief has lived, and will live in our hearts, always. The answer is engraved on the wall in the Congressional Library at Washington. It reads:

"As one lamp lighteth another
Nor grows less
So nobleness enkindleth
Nobleness."

Gifford Pinchot was our lamp, and his nobleness enkindled nobleness.

To the truth of these statements I am glad to sign my name at Brighton, Massachusetts, December twenty-seven, nineteen hundred thirty-nine.

Agnes Veronica Scannell

1615 Rhode Island Ave., N.W.,
Washington, D.C.,
January 5, 1940.

Miss Agnes V. Scannell,
715 Cambridge St.,
Brighton, Massachusetts.

Dear Miss Scannell:

I have read with the keenest interest and great
appreciation the mater-
ial you were good enough to send me. My
best thanks to you for what you have told.
The only fault I have to find with it is
that you have given me far more credit than
I even begin to have a right to.

Happy New Year, and with renewed thanks,

Sincerely yours,

GP

H.J. Tompkins

chapter 11

Frank Tompkins

TENNESSEE, MAINE, TEXAS
1901-

"Your splendid example of honesty and devotion to duty
was an inspiration to scores of men who worked under you."

Frank Tompkins

H.J. Tompkins

ARKANSAS, CALIFORNIA
1902-

"Particularly I liked the spice of adventure in beating
bad weather. Rough trails, swift water. I delight in good
instruments and have been able to make many minor
improvements in the standard equipment."

H.J. Tompkins

Frank Tompkins and H.J. Tompkins, known as Harry, were brothers. Both started out in the U.S. Forest Service at about the same time, 1901 and 1902, respectively. We know very little about their interactions over the course of their careers except for one reference in a letter from Frank Tompkins to Gifford Pinchot noting that it was because of his brother, Harry, that Frank thought "it was wrong to withhold sincere admiration since everybody needed a little "bucking up" in life."

In his letter of December, 1937, Harry Tompkins wrote Pinchot that he discovered that indoor work was not good for his health. He enrolled at forestry school "on Vanderbilt's thirty thousand acres," followed by graduate work at New York State Technical College where classmates and teachers proved to be an inspiration. Later, while serving in Washington, D.C., Tompkins went to see "the Forester" about the possibility of becoming a Forest Supervisor. "I can see his amused smile," he wrote. "However he sent me as Technical Assistant to Chas H. Shinn." His wife had never been west of Virginia.

Posted to California's Sierra National Forest for "four happy years," Tompkins described the trials, tribulations, successes, and failures while Assistant to Forest Supervisor Shinn. He made note of the fact that Mrs. Shinn had been extremely welcoming to his wife, referring to her in a letter as a "Forest Daughter."

As Pinchot had requested, Tompkins described why he had gone into forestry, his day to day work, the obstacles he encountered, and the innovations and solutions he helped advance. In addition, he provided a fascinating description of an important moment of transition as maps replaced boundary descriptions in Forest Reserve proclamations.

At the end of his narrative, Tompkins reveals a sense of satisfaction in "just measuring streams."

420 Broadway
Helena, Montana
March 6, 1940

Dear Mr. Pinchot:

My long delay in answering your letter might tend to
indicate a lack of appreciation for your remembering me
all these years, but such is by no means the case.

I had the misfortune to have a car fall on the back of
my head (while working under it) and about the same time
your letter came I was leaving for surgical treatment.
Then I went to Portland, Oregon, (not wishing to slight
any part of our great nation) and have just returned from
there. On the word of three or four high-class surgeons, I
may expect plenty of "fun" for five or six weeks and then
if everything goes o.k., be very nearly as good as new.

If that is not too late I shall be more than pleased
to start writing an account of my days with the Service.
In so doing, however, it will be necessary that I depend
entirely on recollection since all my of my diaries of
those days were lost when my trunk was stolen from my
storage in Somerville, Texas; shortly after I left the
Service. I would have no difficulty in remembering most
of the men I worked with and in general what went on but
could not be exact as to dates. I can well recall that I
started Feb. 1, 1901, at Washington, D.C., went that summer
to Tennessee with a party led by Fritz Olmstead; the next
summer to Maine under Bill Hodge, and that fall to Texas
under Tom Sherrard, etc.

My brother, Harry, always said that it was wrong to
withhold sincere admiration since everybody needed a

*"My room, at home, Troy, N.Y. when I was a boy and
my cousin Walter E. Irving. About 1888."*
From the narrative of H.J. Tompkins. Library of Congress. Manuscript Division.
Gifford Pinchot Collection. Old Timers Collection.

little "bucking up" in life. Acting on that impulse, I must
say that I have followed your career with great interest.
I was pleased when you attained the Governorship of
Pennsylvania and disappointed when it did not develop
into an even higher honor. This I do know--that your
splendid example of honesty and devotion to duty was an
inspiration to scores of men who worked under you, and I
have always been very proud of the fact that you were my
chief for several years and that we were really friends.

Sincerely yours,

Frank Tompkins

1615 Rhode Island Ave., N.W.
Washington, D.C.,
March 9, 1940

Mr. Frank Tompkins,
420 Broadway,
Helena, Montana.

Dear Tompkins:

Best thanks for yours of March 6. I am awfully
sorry to hear of your accident, and I do hope you will give
yourself time to get well. Whenever you are able to write
the account of your days with the Service, it will not be
too late.

What you have to tell will be most valuable,
diaries or no diaries.

And I do greatly appreciate what you say about me.
As a matter of cold feet, the credit all goes to the men and
women of the Forest Service. There never were any finer
people since Noah came out of the Ark.

Yours as always,

GP

SOME NOTES BY H.J. TOMPKINS

Dec. 1937

My people were manufacturers so I started work
in the factory. Evidently indoor work was not good for
my health. The doctor suggested Colorado. I recovered
and came back to Troy N.Y. and started a small machine
shop. Ill health again. I went to the mountains of North
Carolina and worked as repair or "trouble man" in a saw
mill. Dr. Schenck conducted a Forest school near by on
Vanderbilt's thirty thousand acres. He advised that I
consult Dr. B.E. Fernow at the New York State College of
Forestry, Cornell University. Dr. Fernow allowed me to
take graduate work. I was there one year. Philibert Roth

"Pettis, Foley, Chapman and Clement in camp
Pine Bluff, Arkansas 1901"
From the narrative of H.J. Tompkins. Library of Congress. Manuscript Division.
Gifford Pinchot Collection. Old Timers Collection.

and Dr. John Gifford were very helpful. Among my fellow students were Raphael Zon, Ralph Bryant, C.R. Pettis, R.H. Charlton, Hugh Curran, Anson Cahoon. I am trying to be brief but cannot omit saying how fine and generous was the help received from Dr. Fernow and his boy.

I tried the examinations for student assistant ($25 per month and board while in the field) one job was near Pine Bluff Arkansas in a party headed by F.E. Olmsted assisted by John Foley and C.R. Pettis. Fever caught us. One man died. We were shipped north. Another died soon after. Ticks, chiggers, mosquitos and bad water.

In 1903 Albert F. Porter was in charge of examinations of lands for proposed Forest Reserves in California. Dr. Porter, Wm. Hodge and myself were to help. My allotments were the Feather River, Diamond Mountain, and Lassen Peak. The areas were large and rough and we were to complete the examinations in one season. I worked alone. Much of the country had to be covered with saddle horse and pack horse. I enjoyed it hugely.

Back in Washington it was the custom to make a written description of the proposed boundaries for the President's signature. We decided that a map would be much better in every way. I enclose the original document in which we abolished the written descriptions to the great satisfactions of all concerned. Should this be considered suitable for the Forest museum I would like to have it there.

When the Forester was placed in charge of the Forest Reserves I learned that my ( ) wanted to be Forest Supervisors. I too went to see Mr. Pinchot and asked to be a Supervisor. I can see his amused smile. However he sent me as Technical Assistant to Forest Supervisor Chas. H. Shinn. My wife was a Washington girl (age 24). She had never been west of Virginia.

We reached North Fork after dark at the end of a long interesting but tiring ride on a horse stage. Mr.

"General Land Office. Division "R". Forest Reserves.
R.H. Charlton. About 1903."

From the narrative of H.J. Tompkins. Library of Congress. Manuscript Division.
Gifford Pinchot Collection. Old Timers Collection.

Shinn with his buck board and lively team rushed us up
the ridge to his comfortable cabin where Mrs. Shinn had a
hot supper waiting. The warm welcome has lasted through
the years. My wife had a letter from Mrs. Shinn yesterday
addressed to her "Forest Daughter."

We were on the "Old Sierra" four happy years.
Poor Mr. Shinn! He had expected or at least hoped for an

assistant who was experienced in his problems. Timber sales, grazing, mining, fire fighting. Office records. I confessed lacking experience and he was disappointed but with his friendly help and the help of Mrs. Shinn and the rangers and other forest folks we tackled the problems as they came along.

One that bothered was reports on proposed water power developments. We could get no data on the amount of water carried by our streams. Mr. Shinn wrote to the U.S. Geological Survey Office asking for the loan of measurement instruments. The answer was "no." Then I offered to get some rough measurements. Every ranger was busy. We hired Bob Langworthy a famous guide. Bob and I tied on the packs and rode up one side of the San Joaquin River measuring every tributary and the main stream where ever we could find a suitable section. We used pine cones or driftwood for floats, a tape measure and a stick which we graduated for a wading rod. I used my pocket watch for timing the floats. It was in the Fall of the years we had to get through before the storms arrived. We brought home the approximate minimum flow for all the main San Joaquin waters. Since we had no bridges, cables or waders Bob stripped and waded the icy waters which were sometimes deep and swift.

When I came to the Sierra Forest there were no regular observers at look out points for reporting fires. Supervisor Shinn felt that he did not have men or money that could be spared for this purpose.

The best we could do was to send a man to the nearest high ridge or point for a few hours. Most of the rangers believed even this was time that could be better used on other pressing jobs. As I remember Shut-Eye Mountain got the first permanent Lookout shelter. Among the photos are two. One of the shelter and one of the snow drift which furnished the observer with water.

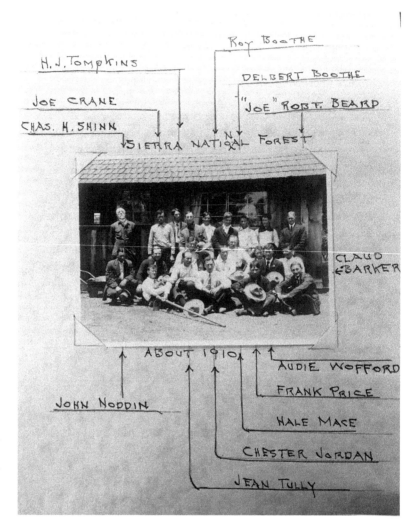

Sierra National Forest Rangers. By H.J.Tompkins.
From the narrative of H.J. Tompkins. Library of Congress. Manuscript Division.
Gifford Pinchot Collection. Old Timers Collection.

Of course we had few bridges at first. I enclose
two views of the Italian Bar Bridge. This was ranger built
cable suspension and cut to one fourth or less the time
on trail from north fork to our important Shaver Ranger
District. The narrow swaying suspension bridge was not
usable for cattle and we built timber bridges of which I
enclose some photos. Hale Mace and Chester Jordan were
often in charge of bridge building in the "back country."
I also enclose pictures of Mace and Jordan always my
staunch friends.

"Snow bank used for water supply for Shuteye fire outlook.
Sierra National Forest Northfork, California. May 20, 1910.
Taken for E.S. Bruce by H.J. Tompkins,"
US Department of Agriculture Forest Service.

From the narrative of H.J. Tompkins. Library of Congress. Manuscript Division.
Gifford Pinchot Collection. Old Timers Collection.

*"About 1925. Forest Service weather station Sister Elsie Peak.
Ele. 5,000 Ft. Angeles Forest. Calif. Thermograph, and
Marvin Glock Rain Gage. Serviced weekly. Seven mile foot trail.
Instrument shelter only. Observer exposed for the whole fourteen miles
including servicing then a tent which blew away. Another tent burned.
Then a 7' x 7' wood cabin. Now a modern shelter with excellent
instruments. 1916–1937. H.J. Tompkins."*

From the narrative of H.J. Tompkins. Library of Congress. Manuscript Division.
Gifford Pinchot Collection. Old Timers Collection.

"Sierra National Forest. Italian Bar Trail Bridge. Built by the Ranger when Chas. W. Shinn was Supervisor with abundant motion vertical and horizontal it was a nervous job to get some horses across. Some would bolt and others squat down. Yet it was a very useful bridge saving much time between North Fork and Shaver."

From the narrative of H.J. Tompkins. Library of Congress. Manuscript Division. Gifford Pinchot Collection. Old Timers Collection.

When the press of engineering work brought us Civil Engineers the need for stream measurements encouraged a cooperative agreement with the Water Resource Branch of the U.S. Geological Survey and I was assigned to that work with headquarters at San Francisco. The work suited me and I measured streams up to the time of my forced retirement at seventy years, 1937.

Some reasons for my satisfaction in just measuring streams.

I believe it is necessary work.

My chiefs both in the Forest Service and in the Geological Survey were always friendly and helpful.

I like travel.

I have had good health.

Sierra National Forest North Fork. Planting Sugar Pine Seedlings
(long root). Chester Jordan (left). Hale Mace (right).
From the narrative of H.J. Tompkins. Library of Congress. Manuscript Division.
Gifford Pinchot Collection. Old Timers Collection.

Particularly I liked the spice of adventure in beating bad weather, rough trails, swift water. I delight in good instruments and have been able to make many minor improvements in the standard equipment.

My wife and our girls were always helping us. Fortunately they were often able to accompany me on short trips in the "Model T," on horseback or on foot.

It is a deep satisfaction to know that our girls (we have no boys) love the mountains and the Forest and have a real affection for all wild life except Mr. Rattlesnake and even he is regarded with respect not horror.

DIAGRAM PROCLAMATION

Reasons for substituting a diagram in place of a written boundary description in Forest Reserve Proclamations.

Gain in Accuracy

Secured by using the mechanical perfection of photographic methods in place of the laborious copy of pencil and typewriter.

Economic Gains

Secured by dispensing with the translation of the diagram (map) boundaries into a written description and then the copying by typewriter and finally by printing and then retranslation of the printed proclamation into a duplicate of the original diagram! The place of beginning!

Gain in Prestige

Secured by Forest Service promptly furnishing any applicant with a clear diagram of Forest Reserve in which he is interested. A messenger could attend to the diagram where it now requires a draftsman and some one to be sure the draftsman has the boundary correct.

In the opinion of Mr. Woodruff the substitution of a diagram for the written description of a forest reserve boundary is legal.

Indian Reservations have been so created by executive order. * (Pyramid Lake or Truckee and Walker

Rivers Indian Reservations. P. 70 & 71 "Executive orders relating to Indian Affairs.")

In order to be certain that all parts of reserve boundary descriptions can be plainly indicated on a diagram a list of the elements of boundaries used in the existing (84) forest reserve proclamations is given below.

Natural Boundaries

Creeks

Rivers

Middle of the Channel of,
Right and Left Bank of,
Point of Confluence of,

Lakes

Shore Line

Oceans

1. High-water-mark on Coast line.
2. Bays, straits, etc.
3. "Islands and adjacent Bays and Rocks and Territorial Waters."
4. Islands "and adjacent islands to the seaward thereof."

Mountain Ranges

1. Summits of
2. Summit of the Divide
3. Crest of the Mountains
4. Cleft or Gorge in the granite peak of the Sierra Nevada Mountains, situated &c., &c., and known as the Yosemite Valley, with its branches and spurs."

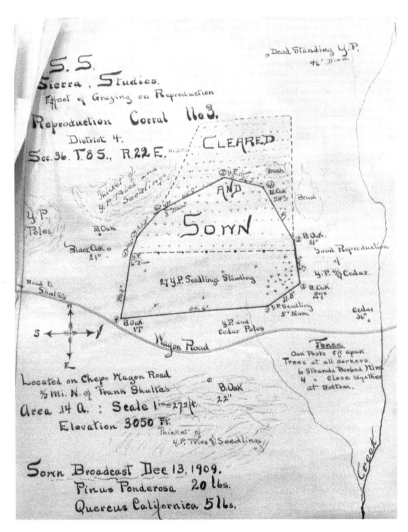

Planting plan by H.J. Tompkins.

From the narrative of H.J. Tompkins. Library of Congress. Manuscript Division.
Gifford Pinchot Collection. Old Timers Collection.

Artificial Boundaries

Parallels of Latitude

Meridians of Longitude

Standard Parallels

Correction Lines

Base Lines

Meridians (Public Surveys)

Range Lines

Township Lines

Section Lines

    1.   Quarter-section lines
    2.   Quarter-quarter section lines

Miles and Fractions thereof

International Boundary Lines

State Boundary Lines

County Boundary Lines

Land Grants (Confirmed and Unconfirmed)

Indian Reservation Boundary Lines

Military Reservation Boundary Lines

Forest Reserve Boundary Lines

National Park Boundary Lines

    It will be noted that with three or four exceptions, rarely used, the diagram would show definitely all of the boundaries now in use. The exceptions can be covered by an enlarged marginal sketch, or by explanatory note in the legend. In the modern proclamation note or sketch would be seldom needed. The repeal of the law allowing selections in lieu has made it feasible to almost entirely avoid the use of subdivisions or sections. However, subdivisions of sections can be clearly shown on a small scale diagram as is demonstrated by the accompanying photograph of the Leadville Forest Reserve diagram of boundaries. Scale 1/8 inch to the mile. * (Leadville proclamation occupies eight printed pages, with the above diagram one printed page is all that is necessary.)

The Preparation of a Diagram Proclamation

The examiner's map of the forest reserve is inspected and if correct, that is, showing boundary facts with reasonable accuracy, a tracing is made. Preferably no topography is placed on the tracing, simply the artificial boundaries which touch the forest reserve and such natural features as form a part of the boundary. The lettering is made large so that it may be clear when the photographic copy is made of about ¼ size. The body of the reserve may be cross-section lined as in the accompanying Leadville diagram, or may be colored so as to photograph slightly darker the area unreserved.

On the margin or the back of this print or on a separate sheet is typewritten the necessary text supplementing but not duplicating the diagram description.

From the same negative a plate will be prepared by photolithography or by the zinc process for printing copies of the proclamation for distribution and for insertion in the statute books.

This last suggests the single objection which has been urged against the use of the diagram, namely, that the State Department and the Public Printer would object to placing maps in the statute books.

The mechanical difficulties are trivial. The diagram can be folded or divided into two or more parts.

The last straw which this administration never permits to stand in the way of progress, is custom.

With Mr. Root as Secretary of State this should be particularly easy.

H.J. Tompkins

*"Sierra National Forest near Ellis Meadow. Sample plot
for excluding stock grazing. Ranger Hale Mace."*

From the narrative of H.J. Tompkins. Library of Congress. Manuscript Division.
Gifford Pinchot Collection. Old Timers Collection.

Afterword

A BALLAD FOR THE ROAD

One enduring byproduct of our earthly struggle is the ballad. Whether spirituals sung by slaves in the fields, chants sung by refugee Vietnamese nuns, or the *ceòl mór*, Scottish laments echoed through the storied hills on the Isle of Skye, ballads have us recall that the human condition is seldom one of luxury but of longing. Songs sung together help us return to the sacredness of life.

When I first stumbled into six tattered boxes of letters at the Library of Congress entitled "The Old Timers Collection," the words of the foresters resonated like music. I felt as though I was being sung to. While digging into how and why these narratives came about and still existed, I learned of James and Mary Pinchot's gift of $150,000 to start a school of forestry at Yale University in 1900. Theirs was not the gift of a building with classical sconces, ergonomic furnishings, and sumptuous grounds. James and Mary Pinchot gave the gift of an idea that impacted the future of the globe: the education and empowerment of a new generation of young people committed to the conservation of nature. As a result of their gift, and Gifford Pinchot's lifetime of service, we have the Old Timer narratives, a record of battles fought, lessons learned, and stories told by young men and women on the ground.

The Old Timer narratives bring us back to basics. As wars, migrations, water and food shortages, wildfires, tornadoes, extinctions, and various forms of violent extremism and militarism plague our cities and homes, millions of refugees wander a warming planet. The narratives remind us of what we long for: not the vast accumulation of wealth or title but service to each other, to community, and to the earth. We need a roof over our heads, a meaningful path to follow, clean water and food, kindness, and the sense that our lives have made a difference to those around us.

The stories in this book present us with more than a dusty old history lesson. They offer a vision that is heartfelt and practical including the skills needed for the road ahead. Pinchot raised a generation of thought leaders who knew how to survive in the woods and how to get along with others. Practical skills taught by the early Forest Service prepared young people for the unexpected. One of the Old Timers, Aldo Leopold, suggested that "a generation must elapse" before the history of the Forest Service could be "truly weighed by anyone."

Gifford Pinchot's early Forest Service offers us a model of cooperation and transformation that we can use as individuals, in communities, or "scaled up" to meet global and cross-border challenges such as the conservation of species, water conservation, and air quality. It offers us a model of domestic civility and foreign humility. We go forth with humility, not braggadocio.

As James and Mary Pinchot gave their gift to a generation

of young environmental professionals, Roosevelt and Pinchot gave a gift to the United States. Without them, there would be virtually nothing left.

Gifford Pinchot said "Conservation is a basis for permanent peace." What if trees replaced wars and weapons? What if we shared the techniques, research, skills, and equipment for water conservation? What if we built greenhouses for cultivating forests and crops? And bridges over surging rivers? What if we gave the communication technology that connects villages to wildlife conservation headquarters to train guardians of nature so that poachers can't poach?

A New Civilian Conservation Corps

The early Forest Service mission was simple: the reforestation of land and the protection of water and other natural resources. That mission is more relevant than ever. It provides the greatest good for the greatest number in the long run.

One innovation of the agency was its architecture, the decentralization of the mission to forest districts. This does not translate into the decentralization of government or the sale of federal land to the states. Quite the opposite. What Pinchot intended was that a small scale version of the Washington Office be set up in each Forest Service Region, and that it be mirrored in each District to effectively manage local resources. The Federal Government would not abdicate responsibility for the master plan or the implementation of its details. It would adjust to meet new circumstances and conflicting resource needs. While many items might be undertaken through agency partnerships, today's challenges are so vast they are best implemented through the agency of government.

A new model of outdoor service—a new Civilian Conservation Corps, on the scale of the Marshall Plan—would reorganize myriad job programs under one roof, providing a model of efficiency and accountability as exhibited in the early U.S. Forest Service. The goal of a re-envisioned CCC would be to train, employ, and equip a new generation of environmental resource professionals including a support staff capable of undertaking a wide range of projects under strenuous conditions not unlike those the Old Timers faced. As public servants, their duty is to be accountable and uphold the public trust. Public servants should be paid a basic minimum income with additional support made possible, at least in part, through housing, food, and equipment allowances deemed necessary to facilitate and fit various project descriptions. Gifford Pinchot emphasized that being paid is not the reason one serves.

Those who will benefit from the opportunities of a new Civilian Conservation Corps model include young people who, like Pinchot's Old Timers, prefer outdoor work over offices. It will serve veterans who need a new mission after returning home from overseas. It will serve the needs of the long-term unemployed who emerge from positions unable to find a job; it will serve college students mired in student debt by relieving them at least partially of encumbrances; it will serve those who emerge from incarceration with the willingness to work by providing them with a job.

From the narrative of Jesse W. Adamson (Served in Idaho 1905-1915).
Library of Congress. Manuscript Division. Gifford Pinchot Collection. Old Timers Collection.

A new CCC will serve the homeless and the hungry.

A re-envisioned CCC provides an alternative to an expensive college education. It would provide job training for the next generation in forestry, animal husbandry, organic farming, woodworking, auto mechanics, plumbing, gardening, horticulture, permaculture, environmental restoration, and construction. It would provide the labor force for public works projects that rebuild and add to existing public infrastructure, including improvements to roads, rail, bridges, multimodal transportation, and improvements to water systems, and America's power grid including alternative energy solutions. It would include improvements to, and development of, additional state-of-the-art laboratories assigned fast-track priorities aimed at energy efficiency and technological advancement. While America transforms its economy and reliance on fossil fuels, a new CCC undertakes massive reforestation and restoration of hundreds of millions of acres.

"Squaw Meadow Bridge, constructed wholly by Forest Rangers.
Idaho Nat. Forest Fall 1912. Rangers Field, Cook + Gaekel."
From the narrative of Jesse W. Adamson (Served in Idaho 1905-1915).
Library of Congress. Manuscript Division. Gifford Pinchot Collection. Old Timers Collection.

Special focus on forestry projects would include the creation of new forests such as what was undertaken on the Nebraska National Forest, and restoration of existing forests. It would provide manpower to address understory fuel loads resulting from long-term fire suppression efforts. Training would include the creation of efficiencies in harvesting and marketing of biomass for alternative energy production. Forest professionals would learn the missions of other land management agencies such as the B.L.M., N.R.C.S., U.S.F.W.S., N.P.S., U.S.G.S., and FEMA in order to be able to better understand and address federal and state issues and disaster preparedness efforts.

A new CCC would create single-focus Research and Development stations (based on early Forest Service Experiment stations) that address issues of high priority such as protection and support of still-intact ecosystems and wildlife. A new CCC would expand the capacity of forest product laboratories for the research and development of sustainable marketable products.

A new CCC would carry on the work of Theodore Roosevelt and Gifford Pinchot by coordinating, collecting, and compiling up-to-date state of the art resource assessments and

*"This was my last fence for the F.S. and the one wherein
I received my permanent injury. Thorn Creek Ranger Station
showing type of timber used to withstand the heavy snows. JA"*

From the narrative of Jesse W. Adamson (Served in Idaho 1905-1915). Library of Congress.
Manuscript Division. Gifford Pinchot Collection. Old Timers Collection.

analyses of existing conditions including forestry, soils, wildlife, and water resources. These assessments and analyses will help determine, as they did in Pinchot's day, where opportunities exist to propose and establish new forests, plant and tree nurseries, and opportunities for water impoundment and retention.

Sometimes I take myself to a cool, dark stretch of river where flocks of the American black duck fly in formation overhead, land for a while, then fly back in the opposite direction. While swimming upstream against the current, I wonder whether we will gather ourselves in time to listen for the sake of the natural world. Extinctions are ongoing. Sea level rise is underway.

The songbird outside my window lets me know that there is still time to listen, but more importantly to sing over the cacophony, despite the rush of modern life and foreboding news of planetary collapse.

One of the joyful moments in discovering the Old Timer narratives was unearthing the story of the "Baked Apple Club," Thursday night meetings held at Gifford Pinchot's home at 1615 Rhode Island Avenue in Washington, D.C. The Club meetings were a treat for hungry young foresters in service to the nation.

Thursday nights were a time to learn, explore, and engage

in discussion on timely topics such as conservation and the management of natural resources for the greatest good, for the greatest number, over the long run. But the meetings did not end there. As the foresters left, they joined together to sing a ballad for the road ahead.

MERRY FORESTERS

'Tis merry, merry foresters we are.
All in this jolly band, sir;
We tramp, tramp, tramp the greenwood near and far,
Passing judgment on the stand, sir;
And if perchance, some lumbering lout
Should injure our fair land, sir,
We'll straighten every error out
By working, working, working out a plan, sir;
We will stock, stock, stock every block, block, block
With a suitable kind of tree, sir;
We are men of knowledge from old Yale College,
To care for the wildwood free, sir.

Chorus

Clink, clank, clink, clank, clink-a, clank-a, clink, clank.
To the forester's life with a forester's wife,
And the woods where each tree is a king.
Clink, clank!

Acknowledgements

I am very grateful for the kind assistance of those who helped make sure that the history of the U.S. Forest Service, as Gifford Pinchot hoped, would be told by the Old Timers in their own words.

Thanks go to the dedicated librarians of the Manuscript Division at the Library of Congress. Special thanks to Jeffrey Flannery, Head of the Reference and Readers Service Section, and reference librarians Bruce Kirby, Jennifer Brathovde, Patrick Kerwin, Lewis Wyman, Frederick J. Augustyn, and Joseph Jackson.

I am indebted to the Forest History Society including president Steve Anderson and historian James Lewis, Andrea Anderson, and Eben Lehman.

Thanks to the staff at Grey Towers National Historic Site including Ken Sandri, Lori McKean, Melody Remillard, and Director Bill Dauer.

Many thanks to the Grey Towers Heritage Association for supporting my research while Scholar-in-Residence.

Special thanks to Gerald Williams, retired U.S. Forest Service Historian, for his sincere encouragement.

Thanks to Betty K. Koed, Ph., U.S. Senate Historian, for assistance with matters pertaining to Theodore Roosevelt and Gifford Pinchot's 1908 Report to Congress.

Thanks to the Simsbury Free Library.

Thank you to John Lamont at the Seattle Public Library Special Collections

Kind thanks to cousins France Willem and her husband, Jean Pierre, for providing a roof over my head while I read the the Old Timers Collection at my great Uncle's drafting desk in my French ancestors' village of plane trees and fountains.

Many thanks to early reviewers James Strock, Dale Bosworth, Linda Buzzell, Curt Meine, and Peter Crane. Thanks to Jackson Eno, Char Miller, Brian and Jan Grimes, and Rebecca Hammel. Special thanks go to my Uncle Tom Gaston and his wife Noni.

About the Author

BIBI GASTON is a Landscape Architect and author. She has provided landscape architecture, site planning, and design services for public and private clients throughout the United States since 1986. She believes in the founding precepts of her profession, that landscape architecture, at its best, reflects a balance between man and nature.

Her first book, *The Loveliest Woman in America: A Tragic Actress, Her Lost Diaries and Her Granddaughter's Search for Home* was published by William Morrow in hardback in 2008 and by Harper Perennial in a paperback edition in 2009. Bibi Gaston can be reached at www.bibigaston.com and www.firstforesters.com.

CPSIA information can be obtained
at www.ICGtesting.com
Printed in the USA
FFHW010640011019
55243985-61028FF